Google Calendar Essentials

Plan Your Life with Ease

Kiet Huynh

Table of Contents

Introduction

1.1 Why Google Calendar?

In today's fast-paced world, staying organized is no longer a luxury—it's a necessity. Whether you're managing a busy career, a growing family, or a packed academic schedule, the ability to keep track of your commitments and plans effectively can make the difference between thriving and just surviving. Google Calendar has emerged as one of the most popular tools to help individuals and teams achieve this balance. But what makes Google Calendar so essential, and why should you use it?

A Seamless, Free, and Accessible Tool

One of the primary reasons for using Google Calendar is its accessibility. As a free tool included in the Google ecosystem, it's available to anyone with a Gmail account. Unlike some premium productivity tools, Google Calendar is fully functional without requiring a paid subscription, making it ideal for students, professionals, and small business owners alike.

Google Calendar is also seamlessly accessible across devices. Whether you're using a computer, a smartphone, or a tablet, your schedule is just a click away. This cross-platform compatibility ensures that your appointments, reminders, and tasks are always synchronized and up-to-date, no matter where you are.

Easy Integration with Other Google Services

Google Calendar doesn't exist in a silo; instead, it integrates effortlessly with other Google services like Gmail, Google Meet, and Google Drive. This integration enables you to:

- Automatically create events from Gmail, such as flights, hotel reservations, and meetings.

- Link Google Meet to events, simplifying the process of organizing virtual meetings.

- Attach documents from Google Drive directly to events for easy access during meetings or tasks.

These integrations eliminate the hassle of switching between multiple tools and ensure you stay productive without unnecessary interruptions.

Versatility for Personal and Professional Use

Another reason to choose Google Calendar is its incredible versatility. It can cater to various aspects of your life, helping you balance work, family, and personal goals. For example:

- *At Work:* Use Google Calendar to schedule meetings, track project deadlines, and collaborate with colleagues through shared calendars.

- *For Family:* Create a shared family calendar to keep everyone updated on school events, doctor's appointments, and vacations.

- *Personal Development*: Use the tool to plan your workout routines, track your reading goals, or set reminders for personal hobbies.

This adaptability makes Google Calendar a one-size-fits-all solution for organization.

Enhancing Productivity Through Features

Google Calendar is packed with features designed to enhance your productivity. Some of these features include:

- *Color Coding*: Assign specific colors to different categories of events (e.g., work, personal, family) for quick visual recognition.

- *Recurring Events:* Save time by setting up recurring events like weekly team meetings or monthly bill reminders.

- *Notifications and Reminders:* Never miss an appointment with customizable alerts that can notify you via email or push notifications.

By utilizing these features, you can tailor Google Calendar to suit your unique needs, ensuring that nothing slips through the cracks.

Simplifying Collaboration

In today's interconnected world, teamwork is essential. Google Calendar's collaboration features make it a powerful tool for both professional and personal collaboration. You can:

- Share calendars with teammates or family members to ensure everyone stays on the same page.

- Invite others to events and track their RSVPs.

- Coordinate meeting times using the "Find a Time" feature, which identifies open slots in attendees' schedules.

These tools make organizing group activities less stressful and more efficient.

Supporting Work-Life Balance

It's not just about being productive—Google Calendar also helps you maintain a healthy work-life balance. With its time-blocking capabilities, you can set aside dedicated periods for work, family, and personal time. By visually mapping out your day or week, you can avoid overcommitting and ensure you have time for the things that matter most.

Google Calendar also enables you to set "focus time" or "do not disturb" hours, signaling to others that you're unavailable during specific periods. This feature is especially valuable in remote or hybrid work settings, where boundaries between work and personal life can blur.

Scalability for Teams and Businesses

For organizations and teams, Google Calendar scales efficiently to meet their needs. Businesses can leverage Google Workspace (formerly G Suite) to enhance collaboration and productivity. Features like resource scheduling, team-wide calendars, and advanced administrative controls make it a go-to solution for managing team dynamics and ensuring seamless operations.

Why It Stands Out

So, why Google Calendar over other calendar tools? While there are many calendar apps available, Google Calendar's key advantages include:

- *Intuitive Design:* Its clean and simple interface makes it easy for beginners to use while still offering advanced features for power users.

- *Cloud-Based:* With your data stored securely in the cloud, you don't have to worry about losing important events or information.

- *Global Popularity:* Its widespread use means it's compatible with many third-party applications, increasing its functionality.

Real-Life Applications

To illustrate its value, let's consider a few real-life scenarios where Google Calendar proves indispensable:

- *For Students:* Keep track of assignment deadlines, exam schedules, and extracurricular activities.

- *For Professionals:* Schedule back-to-back client meetings, track project timelines, and manage team collaboration seamlessly.

- *For Freelancers:* Manage multiple client schedules, set reminders for invoices, and organize personal appointments without conflicts.

Conclusion

Google Calendar is more than just a digital planner; it's a tool that can transform how you approach time management. Its combination of accessibility, integration, and advanced features makes it an indispensable asset for anyone looking to stay organized, productive, and balanced. Whether you're a student juggling coursework, a parent coordinating family schedules, or a professional aiming for peak productivity, Google Calendar has something to offer you.

In the next section, we'll explore how to make the most out of this guide to unlock the full potential of Google Calendar.

1.2 How to Use This Guide

Welcome to Google Calendar Essentials: Plan Your Life with Ease! This guide has been meticulously designed to help users of all levels—from beginners just starting their digital planning journey to advanced users seeking to maximize productivity—navigate the powerful features of Google Calendar. Whether you're here to organize a busy personal life, manage a thriving professional schedule, or balance both, this guide will show you how to make the most of Google Calendar.

1.2.1 Who This Guide Is For

Before diving into the specifics, it's important to understand the intended audience. This book is tailored for:

- *Beginners* who want a clear and straightforward introduction to Google Calendar's features.

- *Intermediate users* who know the basics but wish to optimize their use of time-blocking, integrations, and reminders.

- *Advanced users* looking for creative tips, hidden features, and expert-level hacks to streamline scheduling.

No matter your level of experience, this guide will meet you where you are and guide you toward mastery.

1.2.2 Structure of This Book

This guide is organized into chapters that gradually progress from fundamental to advanced topics. Here's a brief breakdown of what to expect:

- *Introduction:* Explains why Google Calendar is a powerful tool and prepares you to use the guide effectively.

- *Getting Started:* Covers account setup, navigation, and syncing across devices.

- *Event Creation and Management:* Walks through the process of adding, customizing, and managing events.

- *Advanced Scheduling Tools:* Explores reminders, tasks, shared calendars, and collaboration features.

- *Customization and Automation:* Teaches you how to tailor your calendar and automate repetitive tasks.

- *Efficiency Tips and Tricks:* Offers shortcuts, lesser-known features, and solutions to common problems.

- *Work-Life Balance with Google Calendar:* Guides you in using the tool to create harmony between professional and personal commitments.

Each chapter is divided into sections and sub-sections for easy navigation. This structure allows you to jump directly to topics of interest without having to read from cover to cover.

1.2.3 How to Navigate This Guide

To make this guide as user-friendly as possible, we've included the following navigational aids:

1. Step-by-Step Instructions: Detailed walkthroughs with numbered steps will guide you through various tasks in Google Calendar.

2. Illustrations and Screenshots: Visual aids provide clarity and context, ensuring you know exactly where to click and what to expect.

3. Key Tips and Notes: Look out for callout boxes with practical advice, shortcuts, and best practices.

4. Troubleshooting Boxes: Highlight common issues and their solutions, so you won't get stuck.

You can read this guide sequentially or focus only on the chapters that are relevant to your current needs.

1.2.4 How to Apply What You Learn

Reading this guide is just the first step. To fully benefit from the content, apply these principles:

- *Follow Along in Real-Time*: As you read each chapter, open Google Calendar on your computer or mobile device and practice the steps. Hands-on learning will reinforce your understanding.

- *Experiment with Features:* Don't hesitate to explore settings, test integrations, or create sample events. Experimentation helps you discover what works best for your specific needs.

P a g e 10 | 193

- *Revisit Chapters as Needed:* Google Calendar is a versatile tool. As your scheduling needs evolve, you may find certain chapters more relevant than others at different points in time.

1.2.5 Complementary Tools and Resources

To enhance your learning experience, this guide occasionally references additional tools and resources that integrate seamlessly with Google Calendar, such as:

- *Google Tasks* for managing to-do lists.

- *Google Keep* for quick note-taking.

- *Third-party apps* like Zoom, Slack, and Trello that sync with your calendar.

We'll also provide links to official Google resources, online forums, and user communities for ongoing support and updates.

1.2.6 Learning Objectives

By the end of this guide, you will be able to:

- Confidently navigate Google Calendar's interface and features.

- Create and manage events, reminders, and tasks effectively.

- Collaborate with others using shared calendars and scheduling tools.

- Customize and automate your calendar to suit your lifestyle.

- Maximize productivity while maintaining work-life balance.

1.2.7 Tips for Success

To get the most out of this guide, keep the following tips in mind:

1. Be Patient: If you're new to Google Calendar, some features may feel overwhelming at first. Take it one step at a time.

2. Stay Open-Minded: Even seasoned users may discover new strategies or features they've overlooked before.

3. Ask for Help: If you encounter difficulties, refer to the troubleshooting sections or reach out to Google support for assistance.

4. Keep Practicing: The more you use Google Calendar, the more intuitive it will become.

1.2.8 A Roadmap to Mastery

This guide is not just a manual; it's a roadmap to transforming how you manage your time. By the time you finish this book, you'll have a personalized approach to using Google Calendar that aligns with your goals, preferences, and lifestyle.

Let's get started! In the next chapter, we'll begin by setting up your Google Calendar and exploring its interface. Ready to take control of your schedule? Let's dive in!

1.3 Setting Up for Success

Setting up Google Calendar for success is more than just creating events or marking down appointments; it's about optimizing the tool to support your productivity, personal goals, and overall well-being. When you take the time to properly set up your calendar, you create a solid foundation that will help you manage your time more efficiently, reduce stress, and ultimately be more successful in both your professional and personal life.

In this section, we will walk through the essential steps to set up your Google Calendar for success. We'll explore how to tailor your calendar settings to fit your lifestyle, how to create a schedule that maximizes your productivity, and how to integrate Google Calendar into your daily routine so it works seamlessly with your goals.

1.3.1 Create a Comprehensive Calendar Structure

Before diving into the nitty-gritty of managing your time, it's important to build a clear and organized calendar structure. This begins with deciding how to segment your calendar and choosing the appropriate views, colors, and labels to keep things organized.

A. Organizing by Categories

The first step in creating a successful calendar setup is organizing your events into different categories. Google Calendar allows you to create multiple calendars under one account, which is incredibly useful if you want to keep your work life separate from your personal life, for example. By categorizing your calendar, you can quickly toggle between different areas of your life without getting overwhelmed by unrelated tasks.

Here are some common categories you might want to consider:

- *Work Calendar:* Include all meetings, deadlines, work-related events, and project milestones. You might also want to include professional development tasks or recurring check-ins.

- *Personal Calendar:* This is where you can track appointments, family events, personal errands, and any non-work-related commitments.

- *Shared Calendar:* If you live with family members or roommates, having a shared calendar for common events—like family dinners, vacations, or joint appointments—can be a huge help in coordinating with others.

- *Health and Wellness Calendar:* Keeping track of exercise, sleep, or wellness activities can be a great way to ensure you're prioritizing your well-being. Whether it's yoga sessions, workout routines, or meal planning, this category can help keep you focused on your health goals.

B. Using Colors and Labels

Google Calendar offers a wide variety of colors for events. Use these colors as visual cues to quickly identify the type of event you're looking at. For example, you might use blue for work meetings, red for personal appointments, and green for fitness activities. These color-coded events will help you stay organized without having to read through every individual event.

In addition to color-coding, you can also use labels and tags for added detail. For instance, you might add a label such as "Important" for key meetings or "Reminder" for follow-up tasks. Adding these small identifiers can give you more context at a glance and make navigation much faster.

1.3.2 Setting Up Your Time Zones and Preferences

One of the most important aspects of setting up Google Calendar for success is ensuring that your time zone settings are accurate and that your preferences are aligned with your productivity style.

A. Adjusting Time Zones

For those who travel or work remotely with teams across different locations, setting the correct time zone is crucial to avoiding missed appointments or scheduling conflicts. Google Calendar allows you to set your primary time zone, but you can also add time zones for specific events.

To set the time zone:

1. Open Google Calendar.

2. Go to the Settings menu by clicking the gear icon in the top right corner.

3. Select Time Zone under the "General" tab and set your preferred time zone.

4. If you're scheduling an event in a different time zone, simply click on the event's time zone setting and choose the appropriate one for that particular event.

This feature ensures that no matter where you are, your calendar will adjust accordingly to help you manage your appointments and deadlines accurately.

B. Customize Your Calendar Settings

Google Calendar offers a wide range of preferences that you can customize to fit your schedule and work habits. Some settings to consider adjusting for maximum success include:

- *Notification Preferences:* Set up reminders for events, tasks, and deadlines. You can have Google Calendar notify you by email, pop-up, or both. Customize the lead time of these notifications (e.g., 10 minutes before a meeting, 1 hour before, or even a day before).

- *Working Hours:* If you want to avoid scheduling events during personal time or outside of office hours, you can set your working hours. This helps ensure that your calendar remains aligned with your boundaries and prevents late-night or weekend events from cluttering your schedule.

- *Default Event Duration:* Set the default length of events to match your typical schedule. If most meetings are 30 minutes, you can set this as the default, making it faster to schedule future events without adjusting the duration each time.

1.3.3 Syncing and Integrating with Other Tools

A critical component of setting up your Google Calendar for success is ensuring it integrates seamlessly with the other tools you use. Google Calendar is built to work with a wide variety of apps and platforms, from email to project management tools.

A. Syncing Google Calendar with Gmail

Google Calendar is tightly integrated with Gmail, which makes it easy to schedule events based on email invites. When you receive an event invitation via email, it automatically appears in your calendar. Additionally, any changes made to the event (such as time, location, or participants) will update in both Gmail and Calendar, ensuring that you never miss a detail.

To ensure the synchronization works smoothly, check that your Gmail account is linked to your Google Calendar and that you have enabled automatic event creation from emails.

B. Integrating with Project Management Tools

Many productivity and project management tools, such as Trello, Asana, and Slack, offer Google Calendar integrations. This can streamline your workflow by automatically syncing deadlines, tasks, and meetings. By integrating Google Calendar with these tools, you can manage your projects more efficiently and ensure that all deadlines are captured in one place.

For example, you can set up automatic syncing so that your Asana tasks appear as calendar events. This allows you to visualize your project timelines directly within Google Calendar and avoid scheduling conflicts.

C. Using Google Meet for Virtual Meetings

Google Meet is Google's video conferencing tool, and it's directly integrated into Google Calendar. When you create an event with video conferencing enabled, Google Calendar automatically generates a Google Meet link for that event, saving you the time and hassle of manually setting it up.

For virtual meetings, using Google Meet through your Google Calendar allows for easy access to the meeting link and ensures that you have all the necessary details in one place.

1.3.4 Managing Notifications and Alerts

Managing notifications effectively is key to staying on top of your schedule and avoiding missed appointments. While it's tempting to turn on every possible notification, it's important to be strategic in how you set your alerts.

A. Setting Reminder Times

Google Calendar allows you to customize how far in advance you want to be notified about upcoming events. Depending on the type of event, you may want to set multiple reminders:

- *5-10 minutes before:* For short, simple meetings or calls.

- *30 minutes to 1 hour before*: For larger meetings or important events that require preparation.

- *1 day or more:* For tasks or appointments that need considerable prep time.

The key is to tailor the reminder times based on the event's importance and your need for preparation. Too many reminders can create notification fatigue, so find a balance that works best for you.

B. Enabling Custom Alerts

For tasks and appointments that require more attention, Google Calendar also allows you to set custom alerts. For instance, you can set an alert to send you a pop-up notification or email reminder about an important deadline 1 hour before, 1 day before, or even a week before the event.

1.3.5 Maintaining Consistency and Routine

While setting up your Google Calendar is crucial, it's equally important to maintain consistency with your scheduling and review your calendar regularly. An organized calendar that you don't use will quickly become cluttered and ineffective. Therefore, developing a routine around your calendar is key to setting yourself up for success.

A. Review Your Calendar Daily

Make it a habit to check your calendar at the start and end of each day. Reviewing your calendar daily will help you stay on top of your commitments, adjust as needed, and ensure you don't forget important tasks or meetings.

B. Plan for the Week Ahead

At the end of each week, take time to plan for the upcoming week. Set goals, prioritize tasks, and block out time for important personal and professional commitments. By planning in advance, you can ensure your week is structured for maximum productivity.

Conclusion

Setting up Google Calendar for success is not a one-time task—it's an ongoing process. By taking the time to customize your calendar, integrate it with other tools, and establish consistent routines, you'll ensure that Google Calendar becomes a reliable and effective tool for managing your time. Whether you're managing a busy work schedule, planning personal events, or coordinating with family and friends, a well-organized Google Calendar is your key to maintaining balance, reducing stress, and staying on track for success.

CHAPTER I
Getting Started

1.1 Creating and Accessing Your Google Calendar

Google Calendar is one of the most powerful tools available for managing your time and tasks. Whether you're organizing personal appointments or scheduling meetings with colleagues, Google Calendar provides a range of features that make time management easier. In this section, we'll walk you through the process of creating and accessing your Google Calendar, from the very first steps to logging in, to setting up your calendar for the best use.

Creating a Google Calendar Account

Before you can begin using Google Calendar, you'll need a Google account. If you already have one (such as a Gmail account), you can simply log in. However, if you don't have a Google account yet, don't worry—it's easy to create one!

Step 1: Create a Google Account

1. Open your browser and go to the Google sign-up page: https://accounts.google.com/signup.

2. Fill in the required details such as your first and last name, username, and password.

3. Once your Google account is created, you can access all Google services, including Google Calendar.

Step 2: Sign In to Your Google Account

1. Visit https://www.google.com or go directly to the Google Calendar page at https://calendar.google.com.

2. On the top right corner, click on the "Sign in" button.

3. Enter your email address and password, and click on "Next." If you've already logged into your Google account, it will automatically sign you in.

Accessing Google Calendar on Desktop and Mobile

Google Calendar is accessible through a web browser on your desktop, as well as through mobile apps on Android and iOS devices. Both platforms offer a similar user experience, though some features may be unique to each platform.

On Desktop (Web Version)

1. Open your preferred web browser (Google Chrome, Firefox, Safari, etc.).

2. Type in the URL: https://calendar.google.com or simply search for "Google Calendar" on Google.

3. You will be prompted to log in to your Google account (if you haven't already done so).

4. Once logged in, you'll land on the Google Calendar home page where you can begin adding events, viewing your calendar, and customizing settings.

On Mobile (iOS and Android)

1. Download the Google Calendar app from your device's app store. Search for "Google Calendar" in the Apple App Store (for iPhone users) or the Google Play Store (for Android users).

2. Open the Google Calendar app and sign in with your Google account.

3. You will have immediate access to your calendar, with the ability to view, create, and modify events directly from your phone.

Both desktop and mobile versions offer synchronization, meaning your calendar will automatically update across all devices when changes are made.

Creating Your First Calendar Event

Now that you've created a Google account and accessed Google Calendar, it's time to create your first event. Google Calendar allows you to quickly create events, meetings, and appointments.

Step 1: Click on the "Create" Button

1. In the web version, on the left-hand side of the screen, you'll see a large button labeled "Create" or a "+" button. Click on this to open the event creation window.

2. On mobile devices, tap the "+" button, typically located at the bottom right of the screen.

Step 2: Add Event Details

- Event Title: Enter the name of the event (e.g., "Doctor's Appointment," "Team Meeting").

- Date and Time: Choose the start and end time for your event. If it's an all-day event, check the "All Day" box to make the event span the entire day.

- Location: Enter the location of the event, if applicable (e.g., "Room 5B," "123 Main St.").

- Description: Add any notes or relevant details about the event. This is useful for reminders, agendas, or additional context for the event.

- Invite Attendees (Optional): If you want to invite others to your event, type their email addresses in the "Add Guests" field. Google will send them an invite.

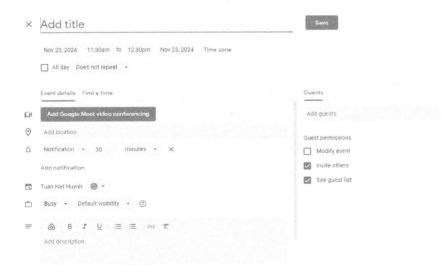

Step 3: Set Reminders and Notifications

You can add reminders for your event so you're notified before it starts. There are several options for reminders:

- *Popup Notifications* on the screen

- *Email Notifications* sent to your inbox

- *Custom Reminders* where you can set notifications at specific intervals (e.g., 30 minutes before, 1 day before, etc.).

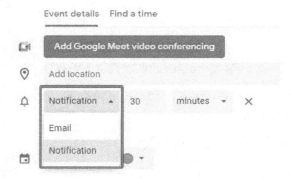

Step 4: Set Event Recurrence (Optional)

If your event is something that happens regularly, you can set it to repeat:

1. Click on the "Does not repeat" dropdown menu.

2. Choose from options like "Daily," "Weekly," "Monthly," or even customize the recurrence for more specific needs.

3. You can set an end date for the recurrence or make it repeat indefinitely.

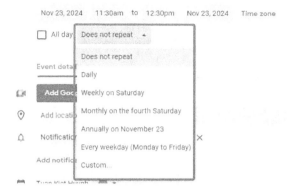

Step 5: Save the Event

Once all details have been entered, click the "Save" button. If you've added guests, you'll be prompted to send them an invitation. You can choose to send the invites immediately or later.

Managing Multiple Calendars

Google Calendar allows you to create and manage multiple calendars. This is particularly helpful if you want to keep your work and personal events separate, or if you're managing a team calendar alongside your own.

Step 1: Create a New Calendar

1. In the web version, on the left side of the screen, scroll to find "My calendars." Click the dropdown arrow next to it, and then select "Create new calendar."

2. Enter a name for the new calendar, a description (optional), and select a time zone.

3. Click "Create calendar," and it will appear on the left-hand side of your Google Calendar.

Step 2: View and Manage Calendars

You can toggle different calendars on and off in your calendar view. For example, you might want to see only your work calendar during business hours and your personal calendar in the evenings. You can also change the colors of each calendar to make it visually distinct.

Customizing Calendar Settings

Once your calendar is up and running, you might want to adjust certain settings to improve how it works for you. Google Calendar offers a variety of settings to enhance your experience.

Step 1: Access Calendar Settings

1. On the web version, click on the gear icon located in the top right corner of the page.

2. Select "Settings" from the dropdown menu.

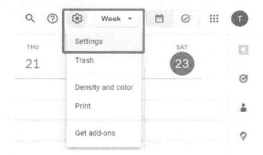

Step 2: Adjust Time Zone and Event Preferences

You can set your default time zone, adjust the start of your week (whether it starts on Sunday or Monday), and decide how Google Calendar displays events. For example, you can choose whether to display weekends or holidays on your calendar.

Step 3: Add or Remove Calendar Layers

If you want to see more than just your own events, Google Calendar allows you to overlay public calendars like holidays, weather forecasts, and sports events. To add these, simply go to the "Browse calendars of interest" section in the settings menu and select the ones you want.

Conclusion

Now that you've learned how to create and access your Google Calendar, you're ready to start using it to organize your life. From adding events and reminders to managing multiple calendars, Google Calendar is a versatile tool that can help you stay on track with your schedule. The best part is that it's fully integrated with the Google ecosystem, meaning you can access your calendar anywhere, anytime.

In the next sections, we'll explore how to navigate the calendar interface, sync across devices, and customize your Google Calendar to fit your unique needs.

1.2 Navigating the Interface

1.2.1 Calendar Views: Day, Week, Month, and More

Google Calendar's interface is designed to provide an intuitive way to visualize your schedule. One of its core features is the ability to switch between different calendar views, allowing users to manage their time in the way that best suits their needs. This section will guide you through the available views, their benefits, and how to use them effectively.

Day View

The Day View is ideal for individuals who need a detailed hour-by-hour breakdown of their day. It focuses solely on one day at a time, displaying your events in chronological order.

- How to Access the Day View:

Click on the "Day" button located at the top-right corner of the interface. Alternatively, use the keyboard shortcut 1 (numeric key) to switch to Day View quickly.

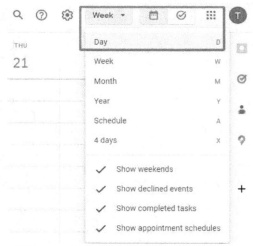

- When to Use:

- Ideal for packed schedules where precision is key.

- Perfect for planning single-day events or managing tasks with specific time slots.

- Helpful for professionals juggling back-to-back meetings or appointments.

- *Features of the Day View:*

  - Displays events in a vertical format with time slots on the left-hand side.

  - Includes event titles, colors, and details like locations.

  - Shows overlapping events side by side for better visual clarity.

- Pro Tip: Use the scroll wheel or touch gestures to navigate through hours if you're looking at a particularly busy day.

Week View

The Week View balances detail and scope, showing you an entire week at once. This is the default view for many users because it provides a comprehensive overview of your schedule.

- *How to Access the Week View:*

  Click the "Week" button at the top-right corner or press 2 on your keyboard.

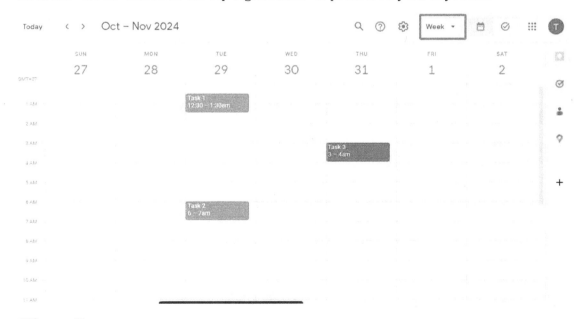

- *When to Use:*

- Perfect for planning weekly goals or reviewing your workload.

- Useful for seeing patterns, such as recurring meetings or empty blocks of time.

- Ideal for team managers who need a broader perspective.

- *Features of the Week View:*

  - Displays events for seven days side by side, with vertical columns for each day.

  - Time slots remain visible, allowing you to see start and end times for events.

  - Highlights the current day for easy reference.

- *Customization:*

  - Adjust the start of the week in your calendar settings (e.g., Monday vs. Sunday).

  - Toggle between 5-day workweeks and 7-day full weeks based on your preferences.

- Pro Tip: Drag and drop events directly within the week view to reschedule them with ease.

Month View

The Month View is ideal for long-term planning and getting a big-picture overview of your schedule.

- *How to Access the Month View:*

  Click the "Month" button in the top navigation or use the shortcut 3 on your keyboard.

- *When to Use:*

  - Perfect for spotting trends or gaps in your schedule.

  - Useful for tracking long-term projects, vacations, or holidays.

  - Ideal for professionals who manage monthly deliverables or personal commitments like birthdays and anniversaries.

- *Features of the Month View:*

  - Displays all days of the month in a grid format.

- Only shows event titles unless you click on them for more details.

- Allows you to scroll through months using the arrows or swipe gestures.

- *Customization:*

- Add public holidays or special calendars (e.g., sports events) to the Month View for better planning.

- Use compact or detailed mode to adjust how much information is displayed.

- Pro Tip: Combine Month View with color-coded events to quickly identify personal, professional, or team-related activities.

Year View

Although less commonly used, the Year View provides a high-level snapshot of your schedule across an entire year.

- *How to Access the Year View:*

Click on the calendar grid icon in the top-left corner or use the menu options to select "Year."

- When to Use:

  - Ideal for annual planning, such as setting long-term goals or tracking milestones.

  - Great for reviewing past performance or planning for upcoming quarters.

- Features of the Year View:

  - Displays the entire calendar year in a single view.

  - Highlights dates with events in bold or shaded colors.

- Pro Tip: Use this view for setting vacation time or reviewing company-wide schedules.

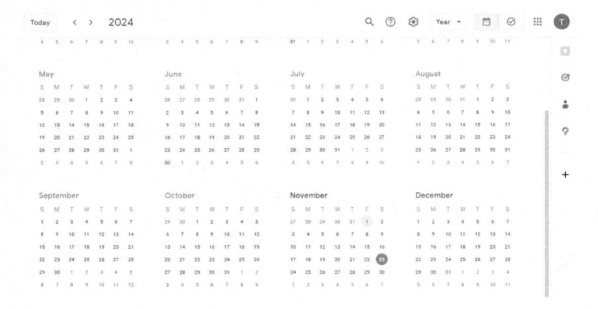

Schedule View

Schedule View focuses solely on your events, displaying them as a list rather than in a calendar grid.

- How to Access the Schedule View:

Click on "Schedule" in the view options menu or press 5 on your keyboard.

- *When to Use:*

  - Perfect for those who prefer a text-based approach to planning.

  - Useful for reviewing event details without needing to navigate through days or weeks.

  - Ideal for printing out a clean schedule for quick reference.

- *Features of the Schedule View:*

  - Lists events in chronological order, starting with the current date.

  - Provides quick access to event details like locations and participants.

- Pro Tip: Combine Schedule View with the search bar to filter specific types of events, such as "meetings" or "deadlines."

Customizing Your View

Google Calendar offers several customization options to tailor each view to your specific needs.

- *Display Density:*

  Adjust your display density in settings to switch between a compact or comfortable view, depending on your screen size and preferences.

- *Color Schemes:*

  Use color-coding to differentiate between types of events, such as personal, work, or team activities.

- *Custom Start of the Week:*

  Choose whether your week begins on Sunday, Monday, or any other day through the settings menu.

- *Multiple Calendar Overlays:*

  Display multiple calendars at once to compare personal and shared schedules side by side.

Switching Between Views

Learning to switch seamlessly between views will make you a power user. Here's how:

- *Keyboard Shortcuts:*

 Memorize view-specific shortcuts (1 for Day, 2 for Week, etc.) to quickly toggle between views.

- *Dropdown Menu:*

 Use the dropdown menu in the top-right corner to access all available views.

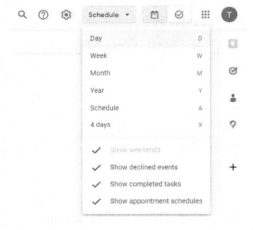

- *Mobile Devices:*

 Swipe gestures on the Google Calendar app allow you to switch views intuitively.

By mastering these views, you can ensure that Google Calendar serves as a flexible and powerful tool to manage your schedule effectively.

1.2.2 Sidebar and Search Functions

Navigating Google Calendar's interface efficiently involves mastering the Sidebar and the Search Functions. These tools are essential for organizing and locating events with ease, whether you're managing a personal schedule or coordinating a team calendar. In this section, we'll explore these features step-by-step, with practical examples and tips to help you make the most of them.

Understanding the Sidebar

The Sidebar is a key feature in Google Calendar that provides quick access to essential tools such as your list of calendars, tasks, and additional settings. It is located on the left-hand side of the Google Calendar interface. Here's a breakdown of its components:

1. Calendar List

- Your Calendars: This section displays all the calendars associated with your Google account. These can include your primary calendar, shared calendars, and additional calendars you've created for specific purposes (e.g., work, personal, or travel).

- Toggling Calendars: Each calendar has a checkbox. By selecting or deselecting these, you can choose which calendars are visible on the main interface. This is particularly useful if you want to declutter your view or focus on a specific area of your life.

- Color Coding: Google Calendar allows you to assign unique colors to each calendar. This visual cue helps you quickly differentiate between types of events, such as meetings, birthdays, or deadlines.

2. Add New Calendars

The Sidebar also offers options to add new calendars. You can:

- Create a New Calendar: Use this feature to set up separate calendars for specific goals or projects. For example, you might create a "Workout Calendar" to track fitness sessions.

- Browse Interesting Calendars: Add pre-built calendars for holidays, sports schedules, or other publicly available events. This feature is particularly helpful for staying updated on important dates without manual entry.

- Subscribe to Shared Calendars: If a colleague or friend shares their calendar with you, it will appear here after you accept the invitation.

3. Task Management

In the Sidebar, you can manage tasks directly within Google Calendar. Tasks are distinct from events and are best used for personal to-dos that don't require scheduling a specific time. For example:

- Creating Tasks: Click on the "Tasks" tab to add new tasks. Tasks can include deadlines, subtasks, and detailed notes.

- Viewing Tasks on the Calendar: Toggle the visibility of tasks by checking the "Tasks" option in the calendar list. Tasks will appear alongside your events for easy reference.

4. Other Features

- Mini Calendar View: At the top of the Sidebar, you'll find a compact calendar for quick navigation. Click on any date to jump directly to that day's schedule.

- Settings and Options: Access calendar settings from the Sidebar to adjust preferences, manage sharing permissions, or customize notifications.

Maximizing the Search Function

The Search Function in Google Calendar is a powerful tool for locating specific events, contacts, or keywords within your calendar. It eliminates the need to scroll manually through weeks or months of schedules.

How to Use the Search Bar

The search bar is located at the top of the Google Calendar interface. Simply type a query, and Google Calendar will display results that match your input.

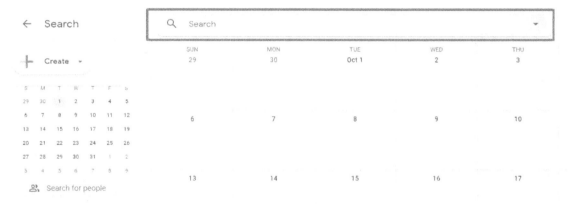

Search Tips and Examples

Here are some ways to use the search function effectively:

- Event Titles: Search by the name of an event. For example, typing "Team Meeting" will display all events with that title.

- Participants: Enter the name or email address of a person to find events where they are listed as participants.

- Locations: Type a location, such as "Conference Room A" or "Zoom," to find events held there.

- Keywords in Descriptions: If you've added detailed notes to event descriptions, search for specific terms to locate relevant events.

Advanced Search Filters

Google Calendar also supports advanced filters to narrow down results:

- Date Range: Use the dropdown menu in the search bar to specify a range of dates. This is useful for reviewing past meetings or planning future activities.

- Calendar Selection: Limit the search to specific calendars by toggling the appropriate checkboxes in the Sidebar before initiating the search.

- Recurring Events: Search for recurring events, such as weekly staff meetings, by using unique identifiers in the event title or description.

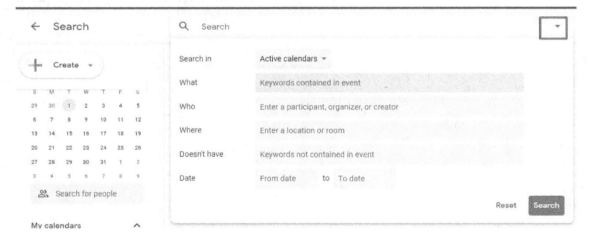

Practical Use Cases

1. Organizing a Team Schedule

Imagine you're a project manager planning a product launch. To quickly find all relevant events:

- Use the search function to locate "Product Launch" meetings across different teams.

- Filter results by date to ensure no overlaps during critical phases.

- Toggle specific calendars in the Sidebar to display only team-related schedules.

2. Managing Personal Tasks and Events

For a busy professional balancing work and personal life:

- Use color-coded calendars in the Sidebar to separate professional and personal commitments.

- Create and manage a "Weekend Tasks" calendar to track errands and hobbies.

- Use the search bar to locate "Doctor Appointment" or "Family Dinner" events without scrolling manually.

3. Planning Long-Term Goals

If you're tracking progress for a long-term project:

- Use the Sidebar to create a dedicated calendar for the project.

- Search for keywords like "Deadline" or "Check-in" to quickly review milestone events.

Troubleshooting Sidebar and Search Issues

1. Missing Calendars in the Sidebar:

  - Check your account settings to ensure the missing calendar is linked to your Google account.

  - Refresh the browser or app to reload the interface.

2. Search Not Displaying Expected Results:

  - Ensure the correct keywords are used and avoid typos.

  - Verify that the relevant calendar is visible and active in the Sidebar.

3. Overwhelming Search Results:

  - Narrow down the search by applying filters for date, participants, or keywords.

Conclusion

Mastering the Sidebar and Search Functions in Google Calendar is crucial for staying organized and efficient. The Sidebar provides intuitive tools for managing calendars and tasks, while the Search Function offers quick access to events and details. By using these features effectively, you can save time, reduce stress, and maintain better control over your schedule.

1.3 Syncing Across Devices

In today's fast-paced digital world, having access to your schedule anytime and anywhere is essential. Google Calendar excels in this area, offering seamless syncing capabilities across all your devices. Whether you're switching between your smartphone, tablet, or desktop, your calendar remains up-to-date and accessible. This section provides a step-by-step guide on how to set up, troubleshoot, and optimize syncing across devices to ensure you're always in control of your time.

1.3.1 Understanding the Basics of Syncing

Syncing ensures that the information on one device reflects instantly on others linked to the same Google account. Changes made to your Google Calendar—whether it's creating a new event, updating an existing one, or deleting something—are automatically synchronized. This happens in real-time, provided there's an active internet connection.

Key benefits of syncing include:

- Real-time Updates: Your schedule is always current across devices.

- Flexibility: View and edit events on the go, even if you're away from your main device.

- Backup: Your calendar data is stored in the cloud, safeguarding against device loss or damage.

1.3.2 Setting Up Syncing on Different Platforms

On Mobile Devices

1. For Android Devices:

Google Calendar is built into most Android devices, making setup straightforward.

- Ensure you're signed in to the Google account you want to sync.

- Open the Google Calendar app.

- Go to Settings > Accounts and Sync > Toggle "Sync Calendar" to ON.

- Events and updates should start appearing within a few minutes.

2. For iOS Devices (iPhone and iPad):

You can sync Google Calendar with Apple's built-in Calendar app or the standalone Google Calendar app.

- Using the Google Calendar App:

  - Download the app from the App Store.

  - Sign in with your Google account.

  - Enable notifications and permissions for the app if prompted.

- Using Apple's Calendar App:

  - Go to Settings > Passwords & Accounts > Add Account > Choose "Google."

  - Enter your credentials and enable "Calendars" when prompted.

  - Open the Calendar app to see your Google Calendar events synced.

On Desktop or Laptops

1. Using a Web Browser:

The easiest way to access Google Calendar on a computer is through a browser.

- Visit calendar.google.com.

- Log in with your Google credentials, and your calendar will load automatically.

- Bookmark the page for easy access.

2. Using Third-Party Apps:

Many desktop applications, such as Outlook or Thunderbird, support Google Calendar integration.

- For Outlook: Use the Google Calendar Sync feature or import events using an .ics file.

- For Thunderbird: Install the Lightning Calendar add-on and connect it to your Google account.

On Smart Devices and Wearables

Wearable devices, like smartwatches, can also sync with Google Calendar.

- For Wear OS:

  - Ensure your watch is paired with your phone.

  - Install Google Calendar on your phone.

  - Calendar events should automatically appear on your watch under notifications.

- For Apple Watch:

  - Sync your Google Calendar to Apple's native Calendar app as outlined earlier.

  - Open the Calendar app on your Apple Watch to view upcoming events.

1.3.3 Troubleshooting Common Syncing Issues

Despite Google Calendar's reliability, occasional syncing hiccups can occur. Below are common issues and their fixes:

1. Problem: Events Not Updating Across Devices

  - *Solution:*

    - Check your internet connection on all devices.

    - Ensure that syncing is enabled in your Google Calendar settings.

    - Force a manual sync: Go to Settings > Accounts > Sync Now on mobile devices.

2. Problem: Duplicated Events

  - *Solution:*

    - Avoid syncing the same calendar through multiple apps.

    - Clear cached data in the Google Calendar app under Settings > Storage > Clear Cache.

3. Problem: Missing Events on Certain Devices

  - *Solution:*

- Verify you're signed in to the correct Google account.

- Ensure the specific calendar (e.g., Work or Personal) is enabled in the app's settings.

4. Problem: Notifications Not Working

 - Solution:

  - Check notification permissions for the app on your device.

  - Go to Settings > Notifications > Enable alerts for Google Calendar.

1.3.4 Optimizing Sync Performance

To make the most out of Google Calendar's syncing capabilities, follow these optimization tips:

- Limit Synced Calendars:

 Only sync the calendars you actively use to reduce clutter and improve app speed.

- Update Apps and Devices Regularly:

 Keeping your apps and operating systems up-to-date ensures compatibility and reduces errors.

- Enable Offline Mode:

 On desktop, enable offline access by navigating to Settings > Offline in Google Calendar. This allows you to view and edit events without an internet connection, syncing them once you reconnect.

- Use Calendar Overlays:

 Combine multiple calendars into a single view to avoid confusion. For example, merge Work and Personal calendars for holistic scheduling.

- Backup Regularly:

 While Google automatically backs up your data, exporting your calendar as an .ics file periodically provides an extra layer of security.

1.3.5 Future-Proofing Your Syncing Setup

As Google Calendar continues to evolve, staying informed about updates and new features will keep your syncing setup robust. Join Google Workspace's community forums or subscribe to their update newsletters to learn about new integrations and improvements.

By following these steps and tips, you can ensure that Google Calendar remains an indispensable tool for managing your time, no matter where you are or what device you're using. Let Google Calendar handle the syncing, so you can focus on what truly matters.

CHAPTER II
Creating and Managing Events

2.1 Adding New Events

2.1.1 Setting Event Titles, Dates, and Times

Adding new events in Google Calendar is a simple yet powerful way to manage your schedule effectively. This section provides a step-by-step guide on how to set event titles, dates, and times, ensuring your calendar remains accurate and well-organized.

Understanding the Importance of Event Titles

An event title is the first thing you see when glancing at your calendar. A clear and descriptive title helps you understand the purpose of an event at a glance.

Best Practices for Naming Events:

1. Be Specific: Use precise language that clearly defines the event.

   - Instead of "Meeting," use "Team Strategy Meeting - Q1 Planning."

2. Include Relevant Details: For example, mention the subject or participants.

   - "Client Call: John Smith, Sales Update."

3. Use a Consistent Format: Develop a standard naming convention for recurring events.

   - Example: "[Type] - [Project Name] - [Action]."

Tips for Quick Access to Details:

- Use abbreviations for commonly repeated terms (e.g., "HR Mtg" for "Human Resources Meeting").

- For collaborative events, prefix titles with keywords like "Draft," "Final," or "Review" to indicate progress.

Setting Dates and Times for Events

Accurately setting dates and times is crucial for effective scheduling. Google Calendar offers several intuitive tools to make this process seamless.

Step-by-Step Guide to Setting Dates and Times:

1. Open the Event Creation Panel:

- On desktop: Click the "+ Create" button at the top-left of the screen.

- On mobile: Tap the "+" icon in the bottom-right corner.

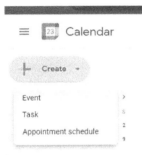

2. Enter the Event Title:

- Type your chosen title in the "Add title" field.

3. Choose the Date:

- Use the calendar pop-up to select a specific date.

- For multi-day events, click "More options" and enter the start and end dates.

4. Set the Time:

- Adjust the start and end times using the dropdown menus.

- Toggle "All Day" if the event doesn't require specific time slots (e.g., holidays or reminders).

5. Time Zone Adjustments:

- For international scheduling, click "Time Zone" to select appropriate time zones for participants in different regions.

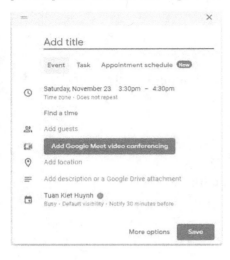

Advanced Features for Time Management

Using the "Find a Time" Tool (available for G Suite users)

- For events with multiple participants, click the "Find a Time" tab to view everyone's availability and select the most convenient time.

Enabling "Focus Time"

- If you need uninterrupted time for deep work, set an event as "Focus Time" by clicking the "Event type" dropdown.

Pro Tips for Efficiency

Keyboard Shortcuts:

Save time by mastering shortcuts like:

- "C" to quickly open the event creation screen.

- Use the Tab key to navigate between fields.

Drag-and-Drop Functionality:

- Once created, drag events on your calendar to adjust their time slots visually.

Common Mistakes to Avoid:

1. Forgetting Time Zones:

  - Always double-check time zones when scheduling international meetings.

2. Leaving End Times Blank:

  - Omitting an end time can lead to overlapping events, which might disrupt your schedule.

3. Not Using Descriptive Titles:

  - Generic names may cause confusion when managing multiple events.

Practical Scenarios:

Scenario 1: Scheduling a Doctor's Appointment

1. Title: "Dr. Smith - Annual Check-Up."

2. Date: Select next Monday.

3. Time: From 3:00 PM to 4:00 PM.

4. Location: Add the clinic's address in the "Location" field for quick navigation.

Scenario 2: Planning a Team Meeting

1. Title: "Team Review - Marketing Campaigns."

2. Date: Choose next Thursday.

3. Time: 10:00 AM to 11:30 AM.

4. Time Zone: Adjust for remote participants in different countries.

Closing Thoughts on Event Creation

Mastering the basics of setting titles, dates, and times in Google Calendar is the foundation of effective time management. By adhering to the tips, tools, and practices outlined in this section, you'll create a clear, structured, and efficient calendar that supports your personal and professional life.

In the next section, we'll explore Adding Locations and Descriptions, ensuring your events are as informative and actionable as possible.

2.1.2 Adding Locations and Descriptions

Adding locations and descriptions to your events in Google Calendar is a straightforward yet powerful feature that enhances the usability of your schedule. By including these details, you not only keep your calendar visually organized but also provide critical information that helps you and your attendees understand the event's purpose and logistics at a glance.

Step 1: Access the Event Creation Panel

To add a location or description:

1. Open Google Calendar on your device.

2. Click on the "Create" button, typically marked with a "+" sign, or click directly on the date and time in the calendar grid where you want to create the event. This opens the event creation panel.

Step 2: Adding a Location

Including a location in your event helps ensure you and your participants know exactly where the meeting or activity will take place. Google Calendar integrates seamlessly with Google Maps, allowing you to choose from a wide range of existing venues or manually enter a location.

Option 1: Using Google Maps Integration

1. In the event creation panel, locate the field labeled "Add location."

2. Begin typing the name or address of the location. Google Calendar will automatically suggest locations from Google Maps as you type.

3. Select the correct location from the dropdown suggestions.

When you select a location, it's linked to Google Maps, providing attendees with the ability to open the address in Maps directly from the event. This feature is particularly helpful for in-person meetings, ensuring all participants can easily navigate to the venue.

Option 2: Manually Entering a Location

If the desired venue is not listed in Google Maps or you prefer to specify a custom location:

1. Type the address or a description of the location directly into the "Add location" field.

 - Example: "Room 301, Building A, Springfield Office" or "Corner Café, Downtown."

2. Double-check for accuracy to avoid confusion among attendees.

Tips for Effective Location Management

- For virtual meetings, consider adding the meeting link (e.g., Google Meet or Zoom) in the location field. This makes it easy for attendees to join without searching through email threads.

- If the event alternates between virtual and physical locations, clearly specify both in the location field or event description to minimize ambiguity.

Step 3: Adding a Description

The description field is where you can include detailed information about the event. This is especially useful for providing context, setting agendas, or outlining expectations for attendees.

Why Add a Description?

- Clarity: Clearly state the purpose and objectives of the meeting.

- Preparation: Help attendees prepare by sharing relevant materials or a brief agenda.

- Efficiency: Save time during the event by reducing the need to explain details verbally.

How to Add a Description

1. In the event creation panel, locate the field labeled "Add description."

2. Type in the relevant information.

   - Example:

     - Purpose: "Team sync to review Q3 project progress."

     - Agenda:

       1. Welcome and introductions (5 minutes)

       2. Project updates (20 minutes)

       3. Discussion on next steps (10 minutes)

     - Preparation: "Please review the attached slides before the meeting."

Formatting the Description

While Google Calendar doesn't support rich text formatting (e.g., bold or italic), you can use simple tricks for better readability:

- Use bullet points or numbers for lists.

- Use uppercase for headers (e.g., "AGENDA").

- Separate different sections with blank lines for better visual appeal.

Step 4: Adding Attachments (Optional)

To make your event even more informative, you can attach files such as presentations, reports, or notes directly to the event. This ensures all participants have the necessary materials on hand.

1. Click the paperclip icon (labeled as "Add attachment").

2. Select files from your Google Drive or upload them from your computer.

Attachments are especially useful for business meetings, project discussions, and study groups.

Practical Examples

Here are a few examples demonstrating how to effectively use the location and description features:

1. Meeting with a Client

  - *Location:* "Café Verona, Main Street, Downtown."

  - *Description:*

   - *Purpose:* "Quarterly review of marketing performance."

  - *Agenda:*

   1. Introduction (10 minutes)

2. Presentation of results (20 minutes)

3. Discuss next quarter's strategy (20 minutes)

- Preparation: "Bring updated sales data and client feedback reports."

2. Team Brainstorming Session

- *Location:* "Google Meet link: https://meet.google.com/xyz-abc."

- *Description:*

  - *Purpose:* "Discuss ideas for the upcoming campaign."

  - *Agenda:*

    1. Review previous campaigns (10 minutes)

    2. Share new ideas (30 minutes)

    3. Evaluate feasibility and assign action items (20 minutes)

  - Preparation: "Think of 2-3 ideas to share with the team."

3. Personal Appointment

- *Location:* "Downtown Gym, Elm Street."

- **Description:** "Weekly fitness session with trainer. Focus on strength training and endurance."

Step 5: Saving the Event

After adding the location and description, review the event details to ensure everything is accurate and clear. Then:

1. Click "Save" to add the event to your calendar.

2. If it's a shared event, choose whether to send notifications to attendees.

Common Mistakes and How to Avoid Them

- Omitting Key Details: Always double-check that the location and description are clear and complete.

- Incorrect Address: Verify the location in Google Maps to ensure accuracy.

- Too Much or Too Little Information: Strive for a balance—include enough detail to inform participants without overwhelming them.

Conclusion

Adding locations and descriptions to your events is a simple yet impactful way to enhance your productivity and communication. With these details in place, you ensure that everyone involved is informed and prepared, reducing misunderstandings and maximizing the success of your events. Whether it's a business meeting, a personal appointment, or a virtual hangout, these features make Google Calendar a powerful tool for organizing your life.

2.2 Customizing Events

2.2.1 Repeating Events and Recurrences

In today's busy world, many events occur on a regular basis—whether it's weekly meetings, monthly bill payments, or annual celebrations like birthdays and anniversaries. Rather than creating new events every time they occur, Google Calendar provides a powerful feature called "Repeating Events" or "Recurrences," which automates the process for you. This section will guide you through setting up and managing repeating events effectively.

1. What Are Repeating Events?

A repeating event is an event that occurs more than once at regular intervals. For example:

- A daily stand-up meeting with your team.

- A weekly yoga class every Saturday.

- A monthly reminder to check your budget.

- An annual family reunion on the same date every year.

Google Calendar allows you to specify the recurrence pattern, making it easy to schedule repetitive events without cluttering your calendar with duplicate entries.

2. How to Create Repeating Events

Creating a repeating event involves only a few additional steps compared to creating a single event. Here's a step-by-step guide:

Step 1: Start with a New Event

1. Open Google Calendar on your computer or mobile device.

2. Click the Create button (the "+" icon on mobile) to start a new event.

Step 2: Enter Basic Event Details

1. Fill in the Event Title, Date, and Time as you normally would for a single event.

2. Optionally, add a Location or Description for more context.

Step 3: Set the Event to Repeat

1. Look for the Does Not Repeat option under the event time.

2. Click this option to open the recurrence settings.

3. Choose one of the predefined recurrence patterns:

 - Daily: The event repeats every day.

 - Weekly: The event repeats on the same day of the week.

 - Monthly: The event repeats on the same date each month.

 - Annually: The event repeats on the same date each year.

 - Custom: This option allows you to create a more specific recurrence pattern (e.g., every two weeks, or on specific weekdays).

Step 4: Adjust Custom Recurrence Patterns (If Needed)

If you select Custom, you can define:

- Frequency: Choose how often the event repeats (e.g., every 2 days, every 3 weeks).

- Days of the Week: Select specific weekdays (e.g., Mondays and Wednesdays).

- End Date: Decide when the recurrence stops—either after a certain number of occurrences or on a specific date.

Step 5: Save Your Event

Click Save to confirm your recurring event. It will now appear on your calendar at all the scheduled times.

3. Editing Repeating Events

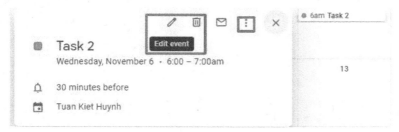

Sometimes, you may need to make adjustments to recurring events, such as changing the time or canceling specific occurrences. Here's how you can handle these changes:

Editing the Entire Series

1. Click on the repeating event you want to edit.

2. Choose Edit Event.

3. Make the necessary changes (e.g., update the time or location).

4. When prompted, select Apply to All Events in the Series.

Editing a Single Occurrence

1. Click on the specific occurrence you want to modify.

2. Choose Edit Event.

3. Make your changes.

4. When prompted, select This Event Only to avoid affecting the rest of the series.

Adding Exceptions

If you need to skip a particular occurrence (e.g., a public holiday cancels a weekly meeting):

1. Click on the occurrence you want to skip.

2. Choose Delete Event.

3. Select This Event Only when prompted.

4. Practical Use Cases for Repeating Events

Work and Meetings

- Schedule recurring team meetings or one-on-one check-ins.

- Add reminders for project deadlines that repeat every quarter.

Personal Organization

- Set daily reminders for habits like exercising or meditating.

- Schedule weekly grocery shopping trips.

Special Dates and Holidays

- Never forget birthdays, anniversaries, or important holidays.

- Plan annual traditions like family picnics or holiday parties.

Maintenance and Errands

- Schedule recurring tasks such as paying bills, servicing your car, or changing air filters.

5. Best Practices for Repeating Events

Keep Descriptions Clear

For recurring events, include detailed descriptions to ensure you remember why the event exists. For instance, "Yoga Class - Bring mat and water bottle" is more helpful than just "Yoga."

Use Color Coding

Assign unique colors to different categories of recurring events (e.g., blue for work, green for personal). This makes it easier to identify them at a glance.

Set Reminders

Enable notifications for repeating events so you receive reminders ahead of time. This is especially helpful for infrequent occurrences like annual appointments.

Review Your Recurring Events Regularly

Over time, some recurring events may become obsolete. Periodically review and update your recurring events to ensure they're still relevant.

6. Troubleshooting Common Issues

Overlapping Events

If a repeating event conflicts with another event:

1. Edit the time or date of the overlapping occurrence.

2. Consider adjusting the entire series if the conflict is ongoing.

Syncing Issues

If recurring events don't appear on all devices:

1. Check your internet connection and sync settings.

2. Ensure you're signed in to the same Google account on all devices.

By mastering the use of repeating events, you can save valuable time and ensure you never miss important commitments. Google Calendar's flexible recurrence settings make it easy to organize your life with precision and ease.

2.2.2 Color-Coding and Categorizing Events

When managing multiple events, appointments, and tasks, it can be challenging to differentiate between them at a glance. This is where color-coding and categorizing events come into play. Google Calendar allows you to organize your schedule visually, making it easier to identify the nature of an event quickly and efficiently. In this section, we'll explore how to use color-coding to streamline your calendar, categorize your events effectively, and apply these techniques to enhance productivity.

Why Use Color-Coding and Categorizing?

Color-coding and categorizing events isn't just about making your calendar look more appealing — it's about improving your workflow and boosting your efficiency. By categorizing and color-coding your events, you'll be able to:

- *Quickly Identify Event Types:* By assigning colors to specific types of events (e.g., work, personal, family), you can instantly recognize your commitments and avoid confusion.

- *Prioritize Your Schedule:* Assigning specific colors to high-priority events can help you focus on what's most important.

- *Reduce Cognitive Load:* Rather than reading every event description, the color of the event immediately tells you what category it belongs to.

- *Better Time Management:* You'll be able to allocate time more effectively by seeing the distribution of your events across different categories.

How to Color-Code Events in Google Calendar

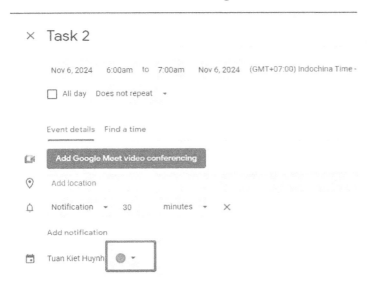

Google Calendar provides a simple but effective way to apply colors to events. Here's how to get started with color-coding:

Step 1: Create or Edit an Event

- Open Google Calendar on your desktop or mobile device.

- Click on an existing event to edit it, or click on an empty slot in the calendar to create a new event.

Step 2: Select the Event Color

- When creating or editing an event, you'll see a color palette next to the event title (this can be seen in both the desktop and mobile versions).

- Google Calendar provides several pre-defined colors, such as blue, red, yellow, green, purple, and orange. Click on one of these colors to apply it to your event.

Step 3: Assign Custom Colors (for Google Calendar on Desktop)

- If you need more color options beyond the pre-set ones, click on the More Options button in the event editing window. Then, select "Choose Custom Color" from the color palette.

- While Google Calendar doesn't yet allow you to create custom color codes in the same way you would in a design tool, the color options provided should suffice for most users. However, you can always use extensions or third-party apps to achieve a more personalized color palette.

Step 4: Save Your Event

- Once you've chosen your desired color, don't forget to save the event so the color-coding is applied.

Categorizing Events for Better Organization

In addition to color-coding, Google Calendar allows you to categorize events by type, adding another layer of organization. Categorization helps you to clearly distinguish between the different types of events in your life, ensuring that your calendar serves your personal, professional, and social needs effectively. Here's how to categorize your events:

Step 1: Use Multiple Calendars

- One of the easiest ways to categorize your events is by using multiple calendars. Google Calendar allows you to create distinct calendars within one Google account. For example, you can create calendars for:

  - Work

  - Personal

  - Family

  - Fitness

- Hobbies

Each of these calendars can be assigned a different color, making it easy to view specific categories of events at a glance.

Step 2: Create a New Calendar for Categorization

To create a new calendar, follow these steps:

1. On the left-hand side of Google Calendar, locate Other Calendars and click the + symbol.

2. Select Create New Calendar.

3. Give the calendar a name, such as "Work" or "Personal".

4. Set your preferred time zone, and add a description if necessary.

5. Once the calendar is created, you can add it to your calendar view. When you create new events, you'll be able to assign them to the appropriate calendar.

Step 3: Assign Events to Categories

- When you create or edit an event, you can choose which calendar it belongs to by selecting it from the drop-down menu. For instance, if you're scheduling a meeting at work, you'd select your "Work" calendar, and for a family dinner, you'd select your "Family" calendar.

- By organizing events into specific calendars, your Google Calendar becomes much more structured and organized. You'll be able to toggle between calendars to view only relevant events.

Step 4: Color Code Your Calendars

- Each calendar can be assigned a different color. To change the color of a calendar, click on the three dots next to the calendar name under My Calendars and choose Settings and Sharing. Under Calendar Settings, you'll find the option to select a color.

Using Event Descriptions for Categorization

Another option for categorizing events is by using the event description field. You can write brief notes about the nature of the event, such as "Team Meeting – Priority: High" or "Doctor's Appointment – Personal". These keywords will help you keep track of events without relying solely on color-coding.

Tips for Effective Categorization:

- *Limit your categories:* Don't overwhelm yourself with too many categories. Stick to 4-5 main categories that suit your lifestyle (e.g., Work, Personal, Family, Fitness).

- *Be consistent:* Consistently color-code and categorize your events to avoid confusion. For example, always use the same color for work-related events and the same for personal events.

- *Use description fields for additional details:* If necessary, use the event description to add any extra context or categorization that might not be covered by your color-coding.

Integrating Categories with Tasks and Reminders

Google Calendar seamlessly integrates with Google Tasks and Google Keep, which means you can incorporate to-do lists and reminders directly within your calendar. Here's how to integrate these tools for better categorization:

- *Google Tasks:* You can create a task within an event and assign a category based on urgency or importance. Tasks can be color-coded and linked to specific events, ensuring you stay on track.

- *Google Keep:* For more detailed notes and reminders, use Google Keep to create notes linked to specific events. You can categorize your notes in Google Keep with labels and colors, which then sync with your Google Calendar.

Example: Organizing Your Day Using Color-Coding and Categories

Let's consider an example where you need to organize a typical day using both color-coding and categories:

- Work-related events might be color-coded blue and placed under a calendar named "Work". This includes meetings, deadlines, and appointments.

- Personal events like gym sessions or family events might be color-coded green and placed under the "Personal" calendar.

- Important tasks could be color-coded red for high-priority and yellow for low-priority.

- Appointments might be color-coded purple and categorized as "Health" under a separate calendar.

With this setup, you can easily glance at your day and see where your time is going, ensuring you balance personal and professional commitments effectively.

Conclusion

Color-coding and categorizing your events are powerful tools for optimizing your time management using Google Calendar. By applying these strategies, you can not only make your calendar visually appealing but also functionally efficient. Whether you're juggling work, personal commitments, or projects, these customization options will help you stay organized and boost productivity.

By using multiple calendars for different categories, color-coding events based on priority, and incorporating task reminders, you will be able to manage your time effectively. Keep experimenting with different combinations until you find the system that works best for you. The more you personalize your Google Calendar, the better it will work to organize your life!

2.3 Editing and Deleting Events

2.3.1 Modifying Event Details

Google Calendar provides an intuitive interface that allows you to easily modify event details once they are created. Whether you need to adjust the event time, update the location, or add additional information, these modifications can be done with just a few clicks. This section will walk you through how to modify the key details of any event, ensuring you can keep your schedule up to date and manage your time efficiently.

1. Accessing the Event You Want to Modify

Before you can make any changes to an event, you first need to find the event in your Google Calendar. Here's how you can do that:

- *On Desktop:*

1. Open Google Calendar in your web browser.

2. Navigate to the date of the event. You can use the day, week, month, or agenda view to find the specific event you wish to modify.

3. Once you've located the event, simply click on it. This will open the event details in a pop-up window.

4. In the pop-up window, you will see an option to edit the event. It's typically represented by a pencil icon or the text "Edit" at the top.

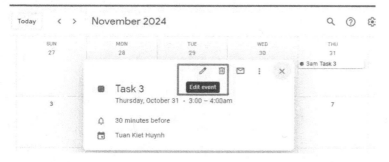

- *On Mobile:*

1. Open the Google Calendar app on your phone or tablet.

2. Tap on the event you want to modify. This will take you to the event details page.

3. You will see the option to edit the event at the top of the page, typically displayed as a pencil icon or "Edit" button.

2. Modifying Event Title

The title of the event is one of the most important pieces of information. It tells you what the event is about and helps you quickly identify the event when browsing your calendar. To modify the event title:

- On Desktop:

1. After opening the event details, click on the event title field.

2. You can now type the new title of the event. Be as descriptive as possible, particularly for recurring events or meetings with several participants, so everyone knows what the event is for.

3. Once you've typed the new title, press "Enter" to save it, or click anywhere outside the field to confirm.

- On Mobile:

1. Tap on the event title field.

2. A keyboard will appear, allowing you to type in the new title.

3. Once you've finished typing, tap "Save" or "Done" to confirm.

3. Adjusting Event Date and Time

On of the most common modifications you might need to make is to change the date or time of an event. This could be because of a scheduling conflict or a last-minute change. Here's how to do it:

- On Desktop:

1. In the event details pop-up, look for the "Date" and "Time" section.

2. Click on the date field to open a calendar pop-up, where you can select a new date.

3. Similarly, click on the time fields (start and end times) to adjust the event timing. You can either type in the time or select it from the dropdown options.

4. After making your adjustments, click "Save" to update the event.

- *On Mobile:*

1. Tap on the "Date" or "Time" field within the event details.

2. You will be prompted with a date picker and time selector.

3. Adjust the date and time accordingly, then tap "Save" or "Done" to confirm.

When you change the time of an event, make sure to check if this adjustment affects any recurring events. Google Calendar will typically ask whether you want to apply the changes to this single event or all future instances if it's a recurring event.

4. Updating Event Location

If the location of the event changes, you'll want to update it to ensure that participants know where to go. Google Calendar allows you to add physical locations or virtual meeting links to your events.

- *On Desktop:*

1. Open the event and locate the "Location" field.

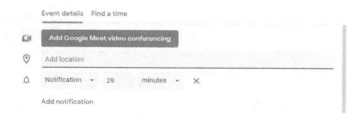

2. Type the new location. If it's a physical address, Google Calendar will automatically suggest relevant matches, including maps for easy access.

3. If it's a virtual event, like a video meeting, you can paste the meeting link (e.g., Zoom, Google Meet) into the location field.

- On Mobile:

1. Tap on the location field in the event details.

2. Type in the new location or link for a virtual meeting.

3. Tap "Save" to apply the changes.

For virtual meetings, Google Calendar can integrate with services like Google Meet, Zoom, and other platforms. By adding the meeting link to the location field, participants can simply click to join.

5. Adding and Modifying Event Descriptions

Event descriptions are essential for providing additional details about the event. This could include agenda items for meetings, instructions for an appointment, or any other pertinent information.

- On Desktop:

1. In the event details section, scroll down to find the "Description" field.

2. Click on the description box and type in your information.

3. Google Calendar allows you to format the text, so you can bold, italicize, or underline important points.

4. Once done, click "Save" to confirm the changes.

- On Mobile:

1. Tap on the description field in the event details.

2. Enter any additional information you want to include.

3. After making your changes, tap "Save" or "Done" to apply the update.

Descriptions are especially useful for meetings and events where details may change frequently or when you need to communicate specific instructions to attendees.

6. Updating Event Notifications and Reminders

Event notifications and reminders ensure you never forget an important event. If you want to modify the reminders set for an event:

- On Desktop:

1. In the event editing window, look for the "Notification" section.

2. You can adjust the time of the reminder (e.g., 10 minutes, 1 hour, 1 day before the event).

3. To add multiple reminders, click "Add notification" and select the time for the additional reminder.

4. Once you've updated the reminders, click "Save" to confirm.

- On Mobile:

1. Tap the "Notification" section in the event details.

2. Select or modify the reminder times as needed.

3. After adjusting the notifications, tap "Save" or "Done" to update the event.

You can also choose to receive reminders via email or push notifications, depending on your preferences and how you want to be alerted about upcoming events.

7. Changing Event Visibility and Permissions

If you need to change who can see or modify your event, you can adjust the event's visibility and permissions.

- On Desktop:

1. In the event details, find the "Visibility" option.

2. You can choose from options like "Default," "Public," or "Private," depending on who should see the event details.

3. If the event is shared with others, you can also adjust permissions for attendees. You can give them the option to modify the event, invite others, or see the guest list.

4. After making your changes, click "Save."

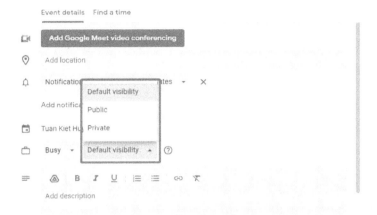

- On Mobile:

1. Tap the "Visibility" field.

2. Choose the appropriate level of visibility.

3. Modify permissions for guests as needed.

4. Tap "Save" or "Done" to confirm the changes.

8. Saving and Finalizing Your Modifications

After you've made all necessary adjustments to your event, don't forget to save your changes. Whether you're on a desktop or mobile device, make sure to confirm the modifications by clicking the "Save" button. If you forget to save, your changes will not be applied, and your event will remain unchanged.

Conclusion

Modifying event details in Google Calendar is a straightforward process, but it's essential to stay organized and methodical when making changes. By taking advantage of the platform's customization features, such as adjusting times, adding descriptions, and fine-tuning notifications, you can maintain a well-organized schedule. Whether you're managing your personal appointments or coordinating with colleagues, these tools ensure that your calendar remains a powerful and efficient way to manage your time.

In the next section, we'll cover how to cancel or remove events when they are no longer needed.

2.3.2 Cancelling or Removing Events

In this section, we will walk you through how to cancel or delete events in Google Calendar. Understanding how to remove events properly can help you keep your calendar organized and free of unnecessary clutter. Whether it's a one-time event or a recurring meeting, Google Calendar provides simple yet effective tools for managing events you no longer need.

Why Cancel or Delete an Event?

Before diving into the process, let's briefly understand why you might need to cancel or delete events:

- *Event No Longer Needed:* Sometimes, plans change, and an event you created might no longer be necessary.

- *Changes in Availability:* You may realize that you or your participants are unavailable or double-booked.

- *Mistakes:* Perhaps the event was created by accident or with incorrect details that need to be rectified by removal.

- *Changes in Schedule:* An event may have to be rescheduled, so deleting or cancelling the original one is necessary.

By effectively managing your events, you ensure that your calendar remains clean, current, and aligned with your schedule.

How to Cancel or Remove a Single Event

Google Calendar makes it incredibly simple to remove or cancel an individual event from your calendar. Here's a step-by-step guide:

1. Open Google Calendar

Start by opening Google Calendar on your computer or mobile device. Ensure you're signed into your Google account.

2. Locate the Event

Browse your calendar and locate the event you wish to cancel. You can use the day, week, or month view to find it. If it's a busy day, use the search bar at the top to search for the event by its name or description.

3. Click on the Event

Once you locate the event, click on it to open the event details. This will allow you to view and edit the event information.

4. Click on the Trash Can Icon

On the event details page, look for the trash can icon, usually located at the top of the event window. Clicking on this icon will bring up a prompt asking you to confirm whether you want to delete the event.

5. Confirm Deletion

After clicking the trash icon, Google Calendar will prompt you with a confirmation message. This step ensures that you don't accidentally delete the event.

- Click Delete to confirm.

- If the event was created by someone else and you're not the organizer, you may only see the option to remove it from your calendar, not to delete it.

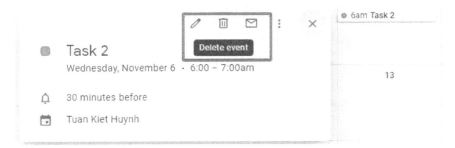

Important: Deleting an event removes it from your calendar permanently. If the event had invited guests, they would receive an email notification informing them of the cancellation.

How to Cancel a Recurring Event

Handling recurring events in Google Calendar requires a slightly different approach, especially when you only want to delete one occurrence of the event or the entire series. Here's how to manage recurring events:

1. Open the Recurring Event

Find and click on one of the instances of the recurring event. When you open it, Google Calendar will recognize that this is part of a series.

2. Choose "Edit"

After opening the event, click the Edit button (pencil icon) to modify the event.

3. Select the Event Series

Once in the edit mode, a prompt will ask whether you want to edit only this instance of the event or the entire series.

- To cancel a single occurrence, select "This event."

- To cancel the entire series, select "All events in this series."

4. Delete the Event

After selecting the appropriate option, you will be redirected to a similar view as deleting a single event. Click the trash can icon, then confirm by selecting Delete.

If you delete a recurring event entirely, Google Calendar will automatically remove all future occurrences of the event. If you remove only a single occurrence, the rest of the series will remain intact.

Note: If the event is part of a repeating series and you only delete one occurrence, the system will update the calendar accordingly. The canceled event will be removed, and the future ones will remain as planned.

Cancelling Events for All Participants

If you're the organizer of an event and need to cancel it for everyone involved, the process is slightly more involved because Google Calendar notifies your attendees about the change. Here's how to do it:

1. Access the Event Details

Open the event on Google Calendar, as you would for any other event. Ensure that you are the event organizer.

2. Click on "Delete Event"

Once in the event details, click on the trash can icon. Google Calendar will give you the option to delete the event and send out notifications.

3. Send a Notification to Guests

After you select Delete, a prompt will appear asking if you want to notify all attendees.

- If you want your participants to know about the cancellation, select Send Cancellation.

- If you don't want to notify them, select Don't Send Notification.

4. Final Confirmation

Confirm your decision to delete the event. Your attendees will receive an email notification informing them that the event has been canceled.

How to Remove Events from Your View Without Deleting Them

Sometimes, you may want to remove an event from your view without deleting it. This can be useful if the event is no longer relevant to your personal schedule but should remain in the calendar for reference. In this case, you can simply hide the event from your calendar view.

1. Remove an Event from Your Calendar

If the event was shared with you but you no longer want to see it, click on the event and select Remove from My Calendar. This won't delete the event; it will only remove it from your calendar view.

2. Hide Calendars

If the event belongs to a shared calendar, you can choose to hide the calendar entirely without affecting other users' access. On the left sidebar, locate the calendar, and uncheck its box to hide the events in that calendar.

What Happens After Deleting an Event?

Once you delete an event, whether it's a single occurrence or a recurring event, here's what happens:

- *For Single Events:* The event will be permanently removed from your calendar, and you'll no longer see it. Any associated reminders, notifications, or other details will also be erased.

- *For Recurring Events:* Deleting a recurring event either deletes just the selected instance or removes the entire series from your calendar.

- *For Events with Guests:* When you delete an event with guests, they will receive an email notification, and the event will be removed from their calendars as well.

- *For Reminders and Tasks:* If you've set reminders or created tasks associated with the event, deleting the event may remove them too. However, tasks set via Google Tasks will remain until they are completed or deleted separately.

Important: If you mistakenly delete an event, there is no "undo" option available in Google Calendar. Make sure to double-check before confirming the deletion, especially for important events.

Common Issues and Troubleshooting

1. Event Not Deleting Properly: If an event isn't deleting as expected, ensure that you're logged into the correct Google account. Sometimes, an event can appear on multiple calendars, and you may need to remove it from each calendar individually.

2. Guests Not Notified: If guests aren't receiving notifications about event cancellations, double-check that you've selected to send the cancellation email when deleting the event. Sometimes, email delivery issues can cause delays.

3. Event Reappearing After Deletion: If you're dealing with a recurring event and it reappears after deletion, verify that you've selected to delete the entire series and not just one occurrence.

Conclusion

Deleting or cancelling events in Google Calendar is a simple process, but it's important to understand how it works to avoid confusion. Whether it's a one-off event or a recurring series, Google Calendar gives you the flexibility to keep your schedule neat and organized. By mastering these cancellation tools, you can maintain a clutter-free calendar, ensure that your events are up-to-date, and prevent unnecessary interruptions to your busy life.

CHAPTER III
Advanced Scheduling Tools

3.1 Using Reminders and Tasks

3.1.1 Creating and Completing Tasks

Google Calendar is not just for scheduling meetings and events; it also allows you to manage tasks and reminders, keeping you organized and on top of your to-do list. By integrating reminders and tasks into your calendar, you can make sure nothing falls through the cracks, whether it's a work deadline, a grocery list, or a personal goal.

In this section, we'll walk you through the step-by-step process of creating and completing tasks in Google Calendar. You'll learn how to set up reminders, assign due dates, and check off tasks as you go. Let's dive in!

Creating Tasks in Google Calendar

Before we start creating tasks, it's essential to understand the difference between events and tasks in Google Calendar. An event is a time-specific item on your calendar, such as a meeting or a birthday party. In contrast, a task is typically something you need to accomplish, but it may not necessarily have a specific time. Tasks are more flexible and can be scheduled at any time of the day, or simply set to be completed by a certain date.

To create a task, follow these steps:

1. Open Google Calendar:

   Go to the Google Calendar website (https://calendar.google.com) or open the Google Calendar app on your mobile device. Make sure you're signed into your Google account.

2. Navigate to the Task Section: On the left-hand side of the screen (on desktop), you'll see an option labeled "Tasks". Click on it to open the tasks list. On the mobile app, you'll typically see a separate "Tasks" section under the "Menu" button.

3. Add a New Task:

To add a task, click the "+" icon next to "Tasks" on the desktop version or click "Create a task" on mobile.

On desktop, after clicking the "+" button, a small task creation window will appear.

On mobile, you'll be taken directly to a task creation page.

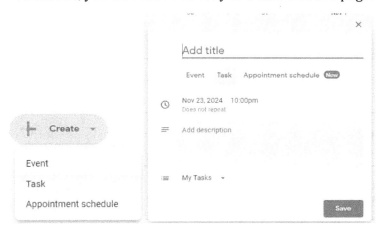

4. Enter Task Details:

In the task creation window, you'll see a place to enter the task name. For example, you can type something like "Finish report for client X" or "Call Mom." This is where you can input the description of what needs to be done.

5. Set a Due Date:

The most useful feature of tasks in Google Calendar is the ability to set a due date. Choose a specific day and time for the task to be completed. If the task is time-sensitive, such as "Call John at 2 PM," you can set the exact time, or you can just set a general due date, such as "Due by Friday."

6. Add Details or Subtasks (Optional):

You can add extra details to your task by clicking on "Add details" or a similar option. This allows you to break your task into smaller sub-tasks. For example, instead of "Complete the project," you can create subtasks like:

- Write project outline

- Review client requirements

- Submit report by 5 PM

This breakdown helps you stay on track and manage larger tasks more effectively.

7. Save the Task:

Once you're done, click Save to add the task to your Google Calendar. The task will appear on your calendar, and you'll receive reminders as the due date approaches.

Completing Tasks

Once you've created a task, it's essential to track your progress and mark tasks as complete. Google Calendar helps you manage and stay on top of tasks so that you can ensure everything gets done on time.

Here's how to mark tasks as completed:

1. Open Your Google Calendar or Tasks List:

To see your tasks, navigate back to the "Tasks" section. You can also view them directly on your calendar by switching to a day, week, or month view.

2. View Your Task List:

On the left side of the Google Calendar screen (on desktop), you'll see all tasks associated with specific dates. You can filter tasks by their due date or due date range, and they will appear in the task list.

3. Mark Task as Completed:

When you finish a task, you can mark it as completed. On the task list, simply click on the checkbox next to the task name. When you check the box, the task will be marked as complete, and it will move to the bottom of your list under "Completed tasks."

On mobile, you can swipe the task to the right to complete it, or click the checkmark icon next to the task to mark it as done.

4. Reopen or Edit Completed Tasks (Optional):

If you need to revisit or modify a task that has already been completed, you can open the task details and uncheck the "completed" box. Alternatively, you can edit the details and adjust the due date if necessary.

5. Clearing Completed Tasks:

If you no longer want to see completed tasks cluttering up your list, Google Calendar automatically hides them after a period of time. However, you can also clear all completed tasks at once. On desktop, click on the three dots next to the "Tasks" label and select "Clear completed tasks." On mobile, the option may be in the settings section.

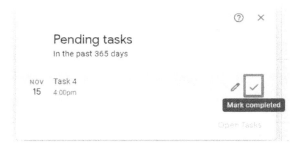

Setting Up Notifications and Alerts for Tasks

To help you stay on top of your tasks, Google Calendar allows you to set up notifications and alerts. You can choose to receive notifications via email or as pop-up alerts in your browser or phone. This is especially useful when you need reminders for deadlines or if your tasks involve multiple steps that require you to stay on track.

Here's how to set up notifications for your tasks:

1. Add Notifications to Tasks (Desktop Version):

When creating or editing a task, click on the "Add notification" button. This will allow you to set how far in advance you'd like to be reminded about the task. You can select:

- Minutes, Hours, or Days Before the Task: Choose how far ahead you'd like to be notified. For example, a reminder 30 minutes before or 1 day before the task is due.

- Notification Type: You can opt for a pop-up notification on your computer or a notification sent to your email.

You can set multiple reminders for the same task if needed. For example, a reminder 1 day before and then again 1 hour before.

2. Setting Notifications on the Mobile App:

On the mobile app, you'll follow a similar process. When adding a task or editing an existing one, tap the "Add notification" option and select your preferred alert method (either a notification or an email).

3. Adjusting Notification Settings (Mobile & Desktop):

If you find that your notifications are too frequent or not working properly, you can adjust them in the settings. Go to the calendar settings by clicking the gear icon on desktop or through the settings menu on mobile. Here, you can customize how and when you receive notifications for both events and tasks.

Conclusion

Creating and completing tasks using Google Calendar is an efficient way to stay organized and meet deadlines. With the ability to set due dates, add reminders, and mark tasks as complete, you can ensure your to-do list is managed and nothing gets overlooked. By integrating tasks into your calendar, you can keep both personal and professional commitments under control, all in one place.

In the next section, we will explore how to share and collaborate on tasks with other users, making it easier to delegate and manage group projects.

3.1.2 Setting Up Notifications and Alerts

Google Calendar is more than just a tool for scheduling events—it's a comprehensive productivity system that can help you stay on top of your commitments. One of the key features that enhance your organizational efficiency is the ability to set up notifications and alerts for both events and tasks. In this section, we will explore how to effectively use notifications to ensure you never miss an important deadline or meeting.

Understanding Notifications in Google Calendar

Notifications are reminders that alert you about upcoming events, tasks, or appointments in Google Calendar. These alerts can appear as pop-up notifications, emails, or even notifications on your mobile device, depending on how you set them up. By utilizing this feature, you can ensure that you're prepared for your day, stay on track with deadlines, and even be reminded about routine tasks.

When setting up notifications in Google Calendar, there are several types you can choose from:

- Event notifications: Remind you of upcoming events.

- Task notifications: Alert you about due tasks and to-do lists.

- Custom reminders: You can create your own alerts for specific needs.

Setting Up Event Notifications

To begin using event notifications, follow these simple steps:

1. Creating an Event Notification

When creating an event in Google Calendar, you can specify when you want to receive a notification. By default, Google Calendar will set a notification for 10 minutes before the event, but you can adjust this to suit your needs.

To customize event notifications:

- Open Google Calendar.

- Click on the event you want to add notifications to, or create a new event by clicking the "Create" button.

- In the event details page, you'll see an option to add a "Notification".

- Select the time when you want to be reminded (e.g., 5 minutes before, 1 hour before, etc.).

- You can choose multiple notifications at different times if you prefer multiple reminders.

Example: If you have a meeting at 2 PM, you might want to set a reminder for 30 minutes before the meeting and another 10 minutes before. This helps you get ready in advance, as well as a quick reminder to not miss the event.

2. Choosing Notification Type

Google Calendar allows you to choose between two types of notifications for events:

- Pop-up Notifications: These will appear on your screen as a pop-up, making them ideal for desktop use.

- Email Notifications: If you prefer a reminder that's more persistent or accessible across devices, you can choose to receive an email alert.

Tip: If you're away from your computer or on the go, email notifications might be more effective since they'll also notify you on your mobile device.

3. Adding Multiple Notifications

For events that require more attention, you can set up multiple notifications. To add more than one notification, click on "Add a notification" after setting the first one.

- For instance, if you have a doctor's appointment at 3 PM, you might want a reminder a day before, one an hour before, and another just 10 minutes before the event.

This multi-tiered approach can help ensure you're well-prepared and never caught off guard.

4. Changing Default Notification Settings

If you find yourself frequently adjusting notifications for events, you can modify the default notification settings for all new events:

- Go to the Google Calendar settings by clicking the gear icon in the upper-right corner and selecting "Settings".

- Under the "Event Settings" section, you'll find options to adjust the default notifications for events you create.

- You can choose to receive notifications for all events by default or customize it for each calendar.

Setting Up Task Notifications

Google Calendar also offers the ability to set up notifications for tasks and to-do lists that you add through Google Tasks. Tasks can be scheduled just like events, and reminders for them are just as customizable. Setting up task notifications ensures that you're reminded of important deadlines and follow-up actions.

1. Creating a Task

Tasks in Google Calendar are integrated with Google Tasks, which allows you to create, manage, and set due dates for tasks directly within the Calendar app.

To create a task:

- Click on a date in Google Calendar.

- Select "Task" from the options that appear.

- Enter the task details and select a due date.

2. Setting Up Task Notifications

After creating a task, you can set a notification to remind you about the task. Here's how you can set task reminders:

- Click on the task in your calendar.

- In the task's details, you'll see an option to "Add Notification".

- You can choose when to be notified about the task, similar to event notifications.

- You can choose from pop-up notifications, email notifications, or even set multiple notifications for a task.

3. Managing Task Reminders

Once a task is set up, you can easily manage its reminder settings:

- If you change the due date of a task, the reminder notification will automatically adjust accordingly.

- If you complete a task early, Google Calendar will mark it as completed, and the reminder will no longer appear.

- You can add additional notifications for tasks that may require multiple reminders.

4. Recurring Task Reminders

Google Calendar allows you to set recurring tasks, and with these tasks, you can set regular notifications.

To set recurring reminders for tasks:

- When creating or editing a task, select the "Does not repeat" option under the task's date.

- Choose a frequency for the task (e.g., daily, weekly, monthly).

- You can then set notifications for each recurrence, ensuring that you're reminded consistently.

Customizing Notifications for Better Productivity

While notifications are a fantastic tool, it's important to strike a balance. Too many notifications can lead to overwhelm and diminish their effectiveness. Here's how to get the most out of your notifications:

1. Personalize the Timing of Alerts

You may want to customize the timing of alerts based on the event or task. For meetings, setting a reminder an hour before might work best, while a task reminder could be more effective with a longer lead time (e.g., a day before).

2. Avoid Overload

Having a constant flow of reminders can lead to alert fatigue, where you stop noticing them altogether. It's important to consider the significance of each event and task and set reminders only for those that truly need your attention.

3. Using Labels and Colors

If you find it hard to distinguish between different types of events or tasks, you can use color-coding in Google Calendar to visually separate them. This can make it easier to identify which notifications are the most urgent. For example, you might use one color for work-related events and another for personal tasks.

4. Push Notifications for Mobile Devices

Google Calendar can send push notifications to your mobile device if you have the app installed. Push notifications are often more immediate than pop-ups or emails and can help keep you informed while you're on the go. Ensure that push notifications are enabled in your device's settings to get the most timely reminders.

Advanced Tips for Notifications and Alerts

For users who want to take full advantage of Google Calendar's notification system, there are a few advanced features to consider:

1. Custom Alert Times for Recurring Events

If you have a recurring event (e.g., a weekly meeting), you can customize the notification time for each occurrence. This can be useful for situations where certain meetings or tasks require more preparation.

2. Using Google Assistant for Voice Alerts

For hands-free reminders, integrate Google Calendar with Google Assistant. This will allow you to set voice alerts and reminders for your events and tasks. Simply say, "Hey Google, remind me to attend my meeting at 2 PM tomorrow." Google Assistant will automatically create the reminder and alert you when the time comes.

3. Third-Party Integrations for Advanced Notifications

Google Calendar integrates with third-party apps such as Zapier, which allows you to set up complex workflows for notifications. For example, you could have a notification sent via Slack or even SMS when a task is due.

Conclusion

Setting up notifications and alerts in Google Calendar is an invaluable tool for staying on track with your tasks and events. Whether it's for a meeting, a personal reminder, or a deadline, notifications ensure that you stay on top of your schedule. By customizing notifications, adjusting their timing, and choosing the appropriate methods (pop-up, email, or mobile notifications), you can ensure that you're always prepared and never miss an important commitment. Keep exploring and experimenting with different notification settings to find what works best for your unique needs, and let Google Calendar work for you in managing your life more effectively.

3.2 Sharing and Collaborating

3.2.1 Inviting Participants to Events

Google Calendar is not just a personal scheduling tool; it's also a powerful platform for collaboration. Whether you're organizing a team meeting, a family event, or a project deadline, Google Calendar allows you to invite others to events seamlessly. This section will guide you step-by-step on how to invite participants to your Google Calendar events, ensuring that everyone stays informed and on the same page.

Why Sharing is Important

Before diving into the technicalities of inviting participants, it's crucial to understand the significance of sharing events with others. In today's fast-paced, interconnected world, collaboration is key to productivity and successful time management. By inviting participants to events, you:

- Ensure everyone involved is aware of the event details, including time, location, and agenda.

- Allow participants to confirm or decline the invitation, providing clarity on who will be attending.

- Enable team members to view and adjust event details, reducing miscommunication and scheduling conflicts.

- Give participants access to event-related documents or links, making it easier to collaborate before or after the event.

Google Calendar offers an efficient way to invite participants while keeping the process simple and organized. Let's explore how to invite participants to your events.

Step 1: Creating an Event and Accessing the Invitation Feature

To invite participants to an event, you first need to create the event on your Google Calendar.

1. Open Google Calendar: Log into your Google account and open the Google Calendar application. You can access it via the web browser at [https://calendar.google.com] (https://calendar.google.com) or the mobile app on iOS or Android.

2. Create a New Event: To create a new event, click the "Create" button (usually marked with a "+" sign or the word "Create" on the left-hand side or at the bottom right of the screen). Alternatively, you can click directly on the date you wish to schedule an event and select "Create."

3. Enter Event Details: Once the event creation window opens, fill in the necessary information, such as:

  - Event Title: A clear, concise name for the event.

  - Date and Time: Set the start and end times for the event.

  - Location: Specify the location of the event (physical or virtual).

  - Description: Add any additional details, such as the purpose of the event, agenda, or any special instructions.

Once you've filled in the basic details, it's time to invite participants.

Step 2: Inviting Participants to the Event

Google Calendar allows you to invite participants in a few simple steps.

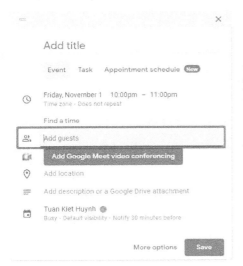

1. Add Guests to the Event:

  - On the event details page, find the "Add guests" section on the right side (on the desktop version). If you're using the mobile app, look for the "Add people" or "Add guests" option.

  - Enter the email addresses of the individuals you want to invite. If they are in your contacts, their names may autofill as you begin typing their email addresses. You can add as many participants as you like.

2. Adjusting Guest Permissions:

Below the guest list, you will see a few checkboxes that let you customize how guests interact with the event:

- Modify event: By default, guests can edit the event, such as changing the date or time. You can uncheck this box if you want to prevent them from making any changes.

- Invite others: This option lets guests invite other people to the event. If unchecked, guests won't be able to forward the invite to others.

- See guest list: Allow guests to view the full list of participants. This can be helpful for transparency, but you may choose to disable it if you prefer to keep the list private.

3. Sending Invitations:

After adding your guests and adjusting the settings, click on the "Save" button. A prompt will appear asking if you want to send invitations to the guests you've added. Click Send to deliver the invites via email. The email will include event details, including the title, time, location, and any notes you've added. It will also provide an option for the guests to RSVP (accept, decline, or mark as tentative).

Step 3: Managing Invitations and RSVPs

After sending out your invitations, participants will begin to respond. Google Calendar makes it easy to track who is attending, who has declined, and who has not responded yet.

1. Tracking Responses:

- Accepted: If a participant accepts the invitation, their name will appear under the "Guests" section in the event details.

- Declined: If a participant declines, their name will be crossed off, and they will not receive further updates about the event unless the details change.

- Tentative: Some participants may choose to mark their attendance as tentative. Their response will be displayed as such, and they may need to confirm later.

2. Sending Updates to Guests:

If there are any changes to the event (e.g., a time change, a new location, or an added agenda item), you can update the event details in Google Calendar. When you save the changes, Google Calendar will prompt you to send an update to the guests. This ensures that everyone is aware of the most current details. You can choose to send updates to all guests or only to those who have not yet responded.

3. Adding or Removing Guests:

If you need to add more people to the event after sending the initial invitation, simply open the event details and add additional email addresses in the "Add guests" section. Google Calendar will automatically send invites to the new participants. Similarly, you can remove guests by clicking the "X" next to their name in the guest list.

Step 4: Managing and Responding to Invitations

As an event organizer, you're not the only one who needs to stay on top of invites. Here's what your invited participants need to do:

1. Responding to Invitations:

When a guest receives an invitation, they can either accept, decline, or mark it as tentative:

- Accept: Clicking "Yes" or "Accept" will confirm their attendance and automatically add the event to their Google Calendar.

- Decline: Clicking "No" or "Decline" will remove the event from their calendar and notify the organizer of their decision.

- Tentative: If they're unsure about attending, they can choose "Maybe" or "Tentative," leaving the final decision open.

2. Managing Notifications:

Guests can set up notification preferences for each event. This can include reminders via email or push notifications, ensuring they don't forget about the event. It's a good idea to remind participants to check their notification settings to stay informed.

3. Changing Responses:

Participants can change their RSVP status at any time. If their plans change, they can go back into the event and adjust their response. For example, if they initially marked themselves as tentative, they can update it to "Yes" once their schedule clears up.

Step 5: Best Practices for Inviting Participants

While Google Calendar makes it easy to invite others to events, it's important to follow a few best practices to ensure smooth communication and prevent scheduling confusion:

1. Provide Clear Event Details:

When creating your event, include as much relevant information as possible, such as the event purpose, any preparation required, and links to resources or documents. This will ensure that participants are fully informed before they accept or decline the invitation.

2. Be Considerate of Time Zones:

If your event involves participants from different time zones, Google Calendar will automatically adjust the event time based on each person's local time zone. However, it's always helpful to clearly communicate the event's time zone in the event description, especially if you're hosting an international meeting.

3. Send Reminders:

As the event date approaches, it's a good idea to send reminders to your guests. Google Calendar allows you to set automatic reminders, but you can also manually send an email or message to ensure everyone remembers the event.

4. Follow Up:

If you're organizing a crucial meeting or event, follow up with participants a day or two before the event to confirm attendance. This helps ensure that no one forgets or misses the event at the last minute.

Conclusion

Inviting participants to your Google Calendar events is a straightforward but highly effective feature that enhances collaboration, improves communication, and keeps everyone on track. By mastering the process of inviting guests, managing responses, and handling event updates, you ensure that your events are well-organized and everyone involved is on the same page. Whether you're managing a business meeting, coordinating a family event, or planning a virtual gathering, the ability to share and collaborate through Google Calendar is an essential tool for modern scheduling.

3.2.2 Managing Shared Calendars

In today's fast-paced world, collaboration and effective time management are key to personal and professional success. Google Calendar offers several powerful tools for sharing and managing calendars, helping individuals and teams stay synchronized and efficient. Shared calendars enable users to view, edit, and collaborate on schedules, making it easier to coordinate tasks, meetings, and events across various platforms. This section will guide you through the process of managing shared calendars in Google Calendar, from creating and sharing calendars to controlling permissions and notifications.

1. Understanding Shared Calendars

A shared calendar allows multiple users to access and manage events within it. This is especially useful in business settings, team projects, or even family life, where coordination is essential. You can share your calendar with others to ensure that everyone is aware of key events and timelines, and you can also manage who can make changes or only view the calendar. Google Calendar allows sharing with different levels of access, giving you complete control over your calendar's privacy and permissions.

2. Creating a Shared Calendar

Before you can manage a shared calendar, you must first create one. If you already have a calendar that you would like to share, you can skip to the next section. Otherwise, here's how you create a new shared calendar:

1. Open Google Calendar:

Go to [Google Calendar](https://calendar.google.com) and sign in with your Google account.

2. Create a New Calendar:

On the left-hand side, look for the "Other calendars" section. Click the "+" icon next to it, and select "Create new calendar".

3. Name Your Calendar:

Enter a name for your calendar (e.g., "Team Meetings" or "Family Events") in the text field provided. You can also add a description and set your time zone to ensure accurate event scheduling.

4. Click Create:

After filling out the details, click "Create calendar" to save your new calendar. Your calendar will now appear under the "My calendars" section on the left-hand panel.

3. Sharing Your Calendar

Once your calendar is created, it's time to share it with others. Google Calendar provides several options for sharing calendars, and you can choose the method that best fits your needs. Here's how you share your calendar:

1. Access Calendar Settings:

On the left-hand side, locate your newly created calendar under "My calendars." Hover over it, and click on the three vertical dots that appear next to the calendar name. Select "Settings and sharing" from the dropdown menu.

2. Share with Specific People:

In the calendar settings, scroll down to the "Share with specific people" section. Click on "Add people" to open the sharing window.

3. Enter Email Addresses:

In the "Add people" box, enter the email addresses of the individuals you want to share the calendar with. You can add multiple email addresses, separating them by commas. If you're sharing with a group, enter a Google Group email address for easy management.

4. Set Permissions:

After entering the email addresses, you will need to choose the level of access you want to grant. There are four permission levels:

- See only free/busy (hide details): The recipient can only see if you're busy or available at specific times, but they cannot view event details.

- See all event details: The recipient can view all details of the events, but they cannot make changes.

- Make changes to events: The recipient can view and edit event details.

- Make changes and manage sharing: The recipient has full access to manage the calendar, including sharing it with others and editing events.

Select the appropriate permission level for each individual, then click "Send" to share the calendar.

5. Sending Invitations:

Once you've chosen your permissions and clicked send, the people you've invited will receive an email invitation to access the shared calendar. They will have the option to accept the invitation and add the calendar to their own Google Calendar interface.

4. Managing Permissions

As the owner of a shared calendar, you have full control over who can access and modify your calendar. It's important to regularly review and update permissions to ensure that the right people have access to the appropriate calendar features. Here's how you manage permissions:

1. Changing Permissions:

To change someone's permissions after they've been added to the calendar, go back to the "Settings and sharing" section. In the "Share with specific people" section, find the person whose permissions you want to modify. Click the drop-down menu next to their name, and select the new permission level (e.g., from "See all event details" to "Make changes to events").

2. Removing Access:

If you need to remove someone's access, simply click the trash icon next to their name in the "Share with specific people" section. This will revoke their permission to access the calendar entirely.

3. Changing Visibility Settings:

If you want to restrict the calendar's visibility, go to the "Access permissions" section in the calendar settings. You can uncheck the "Make available to public" box to ensure that your calendar is private. You can also choose to allow only people within your organization (if you're using a Google Workspace account) to view the calendar.

4. Restricting Event Editing:

If you've given someone permission to "Make changes to events," but you no longer want them to have this level of access, change their permission to "See all event details" to prevent them from editing events. This is particularly useful for ensuring that only a few people can manage critical events.

5. Viewing and Accessing Shared Calendars

Once a calendar is shared, the recipients will be able to access it directly from their Google Calendar. Here's how to view and manage shared calendars:

1. Accessing a Shared Calendar:

- If you've received a calendar invitation, open your email and click on the "Add this calendar" link to automatically add the shared calendar to your Google Calendar.

- You can also add a shared calendar by clicking the "+" icon next to "Other calendars" on the left-hand side, then selecting "Subscribe to calendar" and entering the email address of the calendar owner.

2. Managing Calendar Overlays:

- When you have multiple shared calendars, Google Calendar allows you to view them all at once by displaying each calendar in its own color. This feature is called calendar overlays. You can toggle the visibility of any calendar by checking or unchecking the box next to its name under "Other calendars".

3. Viewing Multiple Calendars at Once:

- Google Calendar lets you overlay multiple calendars for easy viewing. For example, you can view your personal calendar alongside your work calendar or a shared team calendar. The events from different calendars will be color-coded for easy identification. If you want to focus on a particular calendar, simply uncheck the boxes next to the others to hide them.

6. Collaborating with Shared Calendars

Shared calendars are a great tool for team collaboration. Here are a few ways you can collaborate effectively using Google Calendar:

1. Add Comments and Attachments to Events:

   - When creating or editing an event on a shared calendar, you can add attachments, such as documents, spreadsheets, or presentations, that are relevant to the event. These attachments are accessible to everyone with the appropriate permissions.

   - You can also add comments within the event to provide additional details or updates for all participants to see. Comments are especially useful for discussing event details or next steps.

2. Using Google Meet for Virtual Meetings:

   - For virtual meetings, Google Calendar seamlessly integrates with Google Meet. When creating or editing an event, click "Add Google Meet video conferencing" to generate a meeting link that can be shared with all participants. This link will be included in the calendar invitation, making it easy for participants to join the meeting with just one click.

3. Syncing with Third-Party Tools:

   - If you're using third-party project management tools, you can sync them with Google Calendar. Tools like Trello, Asana, and Slack allow for integration with Google Calendar, helping you stay up to date with task deadlines, team meetings, and important events.

4. Setting Up Recurring Events:

   - For recurring team meetings or events, use Google Calendar's recurrence feature. You can set events to repeat daily, weekly, monthly, or at custom intervals. This ensures that every participant is aware of ongoing commitments without needing to manually create new events.

Conclusion

Managing shared calendars in Google Calendar can greatly enhance communication, improve team collaboration, and streamline scheduling. By following the steps outlined in this section, you can ensure that your calendars are properly shared and managed, giving you and your team the tools needed to stay organized and efficient. Whether you're coordinating meetings, managing projects, or simply staying on top of personal events, Google Calendar is a versatile tool that simplifies the scheduling process.

3.3 Scheduling Appointments with Appointment Slots

Google Calendar is not only a tool for scheduling events but also a powerful platform for setting up appointments and managing meetings. One of the most useful features for managing appointments efficiently is Appointment Slots. This feature enables you to allocate specific blocks of time for appointments, making it easier for clients, colleagues, or anyone needing your time to book a session without the back-and-forth emails or messages. Whether you are managing a busy schedule or offering your time for consultations, using appointment slots can save you time and reduce scheduling conflicts.

What Are Appointment Slots?

Appointment Slots allow you to create specific time blocks in your calendar that others can book. These slots can be set for a variety of durations, such as 15-minute, 30-minute, or 1-hour intervals, depending on how long you wish to allocate for each appointment. Instead of having multiple back-and-forth conversations or emails to find a mutually convenient time, Appointment Slots allow others to view your availability and book a time that works for them.

When you create Appointment Slots, you will have the ability to:

- Define the time range (e.g., 9 AM to 5 PM).

- Set the duration of each slot (e.g., 30 minutes).

- Allow others to book within this range without interrupting other events on your calendar.

- Manage who can book appointments with you and how they can access these slots.

How to Set Up Appointment Slots

Setting up Appointment Slots is a straightforward process, but it does require a few steps to ensure that everything is configured properly. Follow these detailed instructions to create your own Appointment Slots.

Step 1: Open Google Calendar

Start by opening Google Calendar in your web browser. You will need to use the desktop version of Google Calendar, as Appointment Slots cannot be set up through the mobile app.

Step 2: Choose the Date and Time Range

Find the date on which you want to begin offering appointment slots. Select the desired day and click on a time that fits within the time range when you are available for appointments. For example, if you are available from 9 AM to 5 PM, select 9 AM as the start time.

Step 3: Create an Event

After selecting your start time, a small event window will pop up. In this window, you will need to select "Appointment slots" instead of creating a regular event. This option will allow you to create a block of time during which others can book appointments with you.

Step 4: Set Your Appointment Slot Details

Once you have chosen Appointment Slots, you will need to configure the following details:

- Title: Give the event a title that explains the nature of the appointments. For example, you could title it "Consultation Appointments" or "Interview Slots."

- Date and Time Range: Set the overall time range when the slots are available. This will be the window during which others can book time with you.

- Slot Duration: Decide how long each appointment will last. You can set each slot to be 15, 30, or 60 minutes, depending on your needs. If you are offering consultations or interviews, 30-minute or 60-minute slots are typically ideal.

- Availability: Ensure that you have blocked out any time during which you are not available, such as breaks, lunch, or other events. This will prevent people from accidentally booking over your non-available time.

Step 5: Add Additional Details

Optionally, you can add a description or any specific instructions about the appointment. This is helpful if there are requirements for attendees, such as bringing documents or confirming an agenda. Additionally, you can set up reminders for both you and the person booking the appointment, ensuring that you don't forget the scheduled session.

Step 6: Save and Share the Appointment Slot Link

After creating the Appointment Slots, Google Calendar will generate a unique link that you can share with others. This link allows people to view the available time slots and book appointments with you. You can share this link via email, messaging apps, or embed it on your website if needed.

To share the link:

- Click on the Event you created for Appointment Slots.

- In the event details, you will see a link labeled "This calendar's appointment slots". Click on the link to copy it.

- Send the link to your clients, colleagues, or anyone who needs to book an appointment with you.

Managing and Customizing Appointment Slots

Once your Appointment Slots are set up and shared, you may want to make adjustments or manage how appointments are booked. Google Calendar provides several options to help you stay organized and control your availability.

1. Customizing the Slot Length

You may find that different appointments require different durations. For example, a meeting with a client may take longer than a brief check-in with a colleague. Google Calendar allows you to adjust the duration of the slots by clicking on the "Edit" button in the event window and changing the duration.

2. Editing Appointment Slot Details

You can edit the details of the appointment slots at any time. If your availability changes or you need to add additional slots, simply open the Appointment Slot event, make your changes, and save the updated event. You can also adjust the title or description if there are any changes to the nature of the appointments.

3. Cancelling or Rescheduling Appointments

If you need to cancel or reschedule an appointment slot, you can do so by opening the event and either deleting or adjusting the time range. If someone has already booked an appointment in that slot, they will receive a notification of the change or cancellation.

4. Limiting Who Can Book Appointments

By default, anyone with the link to your appointment slots can book time with you. However, you may want to limit who can access your slots. This is especially useful for consultations or meetings with specific individuals or teams. You can use the "Add guests" feature in the event details to restrict access to certain people, or you can share the appointment slot link only with selected individuals.

Benefits of Using Appointment Slots

The Appointment Slots feature is an excellent tool for both personal and professional use. Here are some of the key benefits:

- Time Efficiency: Instead of back-and-forth emails to coordinate schedules, Appointment Slots allow others to see your availability and choose a convenient time.

- Control Over Your Schedule: You can manage your availability, ensure that your day is properly structured, and avoid over-booking or double-booking yourself.

- Improved Organization: Appointment Slots help to keep your calendar organized, preventing random or unexpected meetings from disrupting your planned day.

- Clear Communication: When you share your Appointment Slot link, the booking process is streamlined, and both you and the person booking the appointment are clear on the timing, duration, and purpose.

Best Practices for Using Appointment Slots

While Appointment Slots are incredibly convenient, there are some best practices to consider when using them effectively:

1. Buffer Time: Ensure there is enough time between appointments to account for overruns or to give yourself a break.

2. Set Limits on the Number of Slots: Limit the number of available slots per day to avoid overloading yourself with back-to-back appointments.

3. Include Clear Instructions: If the appointment requires preparation or documents, be sure to provide clear instructions in the event description.

4. Regularly Review Your Calendar: Check your calendar regularly to ensure that no conflicts arise and that you are not double-booking yourself.

Conclusion

Google Calendar's Appointment Slots feature is a fantastic tool for anyone who needs to schedule appointments, meetings, or consultations. By offering a simple way to set up and share available time slots, you can streamline your scheduling process and avoid the common frustrations of managing appointments. Whether you're managing personal meetings or professional consultations, Appointment Slots can help you stay organized, save time, and focus on what really matters.

CHAPTER IV
Customizing Your Calendar

4.1 Adjusting Calendar Settings

4.1.1 Changing Time Zones and Display Options

Google Calendar is a versatile tool that caters to users with diverse scheduling needs, including managing events across multiple time zones and customizing the calendar's display for better usability. This section provides a step-by-step guide on adjusting these settings effectively.

Understanding Time Zones in Google Calendar

One of the most valuable features of Google Calendar is its ability to manage events in various time zones. This is particularly useful for people who travel frequently, work with global teams, or manage personal and professional commitments spanning different regions.

Step 1: Accessing Time Zone Settings

1. Open your Google Calendar on your desktop or mobile device.

2. Click the gear icon in the top-right corner to access Settings.

3. Under General, select Time zone.

Step 2: Setting Your Primary Time Zone

- In the Time zone section, you'll see an option to select your primary time zone.

- Use the dropdown menu to choose the time zone where you primarily work or live.

- Check the box labeled Display secondary time zone if you want to see two time zones simultaneously.

Step 3: Adding a Secondary Time Zone

1. After enabling the secondary time zone option, use the dropdown menu to select an additional time zone.

2. Label your time zones (e.g., "Home" and "Work") for easy identification.

Tips for Managing Time Zones

- When creating a new event, you can set its specific time zone by clicking Time zone under the date and time settings. This ensures that the event adjusts appropriately if you're viewing it from a different location.

- Google Calendar will automatically update events to reflect your current time zone when you travel.

Customizing Display Options

Google Calendar allows you to tailor its appearance to suit your preferences, making it easier to view and manage your schedule at a glance.

Step 1: Choosing Your Default View

1. Go to the Settings menu via the gear icon.

2. Under View options, choose a default view, such as Day, Week, Month, or Schedule.

   - Day View: Displays a single day's events in detail.

   - Week View: Shows events for the current week, ideal for short-term planning.

   - Month View: Provides a high-level overview, best for tracking long-term commitments.

   - Schedule View: Lists events in chronological order, highlighting only those with set times.

Step 2: Adjusting the Start of the Week

1. In the View options, select Start of the week.

2. Choose your preferred starting day (e.g., Sunday or Monday).

Step 3: Setting Working Hours

1. In General Settings, navigate to Working Hours.

2. Enable the option to specify your work schedule.

3. Set your start and end times for each day of the week.

4. This feature helps collaborators know when you're available.

Step 4: Customizing Event Colors

1. To enhance visual clarity, assign different colors to event categories (e.g., personal, work, meetings).

2. Right-click on an event in your calendar to change its color, or create a color-coded calendar for specific types of events.

Step 5: Adjusting Density and Display

1. In Settings, locate the Density and color section.

2. Choose between Compact and Responsive modes:

   - Compact mode reduces spacing for a denser view.

   - Responsive mode adjusts automatically based on your screen size.

Tips for Display Customization

- Enable the Show weekends option if you need weekend events displayed prominently.

- Turn on Reduce the brightness of past events for a clearer focus on upcoming tasks.

Practical Use Cases for These Settings

Case 1: Managing a Travel Schedule

Imagine you're a consultant frequently traveling between New York and London. You can set your primary time zone to New York and add London as a secondary time zone. This way, you can schedule client meetings without confusion.

Case 2: Streamlining a Busy Work Calendar

If you manage a calendar packed with overlapping events, setting distinct colors for different event categories can help you quickly identify priorities.

Case 3: Planning Across Multiple Time Zones

Suppose you have a virtual team working from different regions. Use the time zone feature to create events specific to each team member's location, ensuring everyone receives accurate reminders.

Troubleshooting and FAQs

Problem 1: Time Zones Not Updating Automatically

- Ensure location settings are enabled on your device.

- Check that your calendar app is synced and updated.

Problem 2: Missing Display Options

- If certain display options don't appear, verify that you're using the latest version of Google Calendar.

Problem 3: Overwhelming Calendar View

- Use Hide from list for calendars you don't need regularly.

By mastering these time zone and display settings, you can create a personalized Google Calendar experience tailored to your unique scheduling needs. Continue exploring the next sections to unlock even more features!

4.1.2 Managing Notification Preferences

Google Calendar notifications are vital for ensuring you stay on top of your events and tasks. Properly managing these notifications can help you strike the right balance between being informed and avoiding distractions. This section provides a detailed guide to setting up, customizing, and optimizing notification preferences for both desktop and mobile devices.

What Are Notification Preferences?

Notification preferences determine how and when Google Calendar alerts you about upcoming events, changes to schedules, or reminders for tasks. These notifications can take various forms:

- Pop-ups: On-screen alerts that appear in your browser or app.

- Emails: Notifications sent to your associated Gmail account.

- Push Notifications: Alerts sent to your mobile device via the Google Calendar app.

By managing these options, you can tailor notifications to suit your needs and prevent information overload.

Setting Up Default Notifications

1. Configuring Default Notifications for All Events

To manage notifications for all events in your calendar:

1. Open Google Calendar on your desktop.

2. Click the gear icon in the top-right corner and select Settings.

3. On the left menu, choose Notification Settings under your calendar's name.

4. Adjust the following options:

   - Event Reminders: Set a default reminder (e.g., 10 minutes before).

   - All-Day Events: Choose when you want to be reminded (e.g., a day before).

5. Save your changes.

2. Adjusting Notifications for Individual Events

For events requiring unique reminders:

1. Open the event by clicking on it in your calendar.

2. Select the pencil icon to edit the event.

3. Scroll to the notification section and click Add Notification.

4. Customize the type (pop-up, email) and timing (e.g., 15 minutes, 1 hour).

5. Save the changes.

Customizing Notification Preferences for Mobile Devices

Accessing Mobile Notification Settings

To adjust notifications on the Google Calendar mobile app:

1. Open the app and tap the menu icon (three horizontal lines) in the top-left corner.

2. Scroll to Settings and tap your calendar.

3. Tap Notifications to customize preferences.

Types of Mobile Notifications

- Push Notifications: Instant alerts on your phone. Ideal for time-sensitive events.

- Silent Notifications: Appear without sound, reducing interruptions.

Syncing with Do Not Disturb Modes

Most smartphones allow Google Calendar notifications to sync with system-level "Do Not Disturb" settings. Use this feature during meetings or focus times to prevent distractions.

Email Notifications

Types of Email Notifications

Google Calendar sends several types of email notifications, including:

- Event Reminders: Alerts about upcoming events.

- Event Changes: Updates when someone modifies a shared event.

- Daily Agendas: A summary of your day sent each morning.

Configuring Email Notifications

1. Go to Settings in Google Calendar on your desktop.

2. Under your calendar's name, select General Notifications.

3. Adjust the settings:

   - New Events: Get emails when someone invites you.

   - Canceled Events: Receive emails for event cancellations.

   - Daily Agenda: Turn on or off.

4. Save your preferences.

Best Practices for Managing Notifications

Avoid Overloading Yourself

Too many notifications can lead to frustration or even ignoring alerts. To prevent this:

- Prioritize events that require reminders (e.g., meetings, deadlines).

- Turn off notifications for less critical calendars, such as public holidays.

Use Multiple Reminders Strategically

For important events, set up multiple reminders:

- First Reminder: Hours or days before to prepare.

- Second Reminder: 10–15 minutes before to act.

Sync Across Devices

Ensure your notification settings are consistent across devices. For example:

- Use push notifications on your phone for immediate alerts.

- Set email notifications on your desktop for a daily overview.

Troubleshooting Notification Issues

Not Receiving Notifications

If notifications aren't appearing:

- Check Permissions: Ensure your browser or app has permission to send notifications.

- Sync Devices: Go to your mobile app settings and verify that syncing is enabled.

- Restart the App: Sometimes, a quick restart can resolve issues.

Notifications Are Delayed

Delayed notifications can disrupt your schedule. To fix this:

- Update the App: Ensure you have the latest version of Google Calendar.

- Check Internet Connection: A poor connection can cause delays.

Too Many Notifications

If you're overwhelmed:

- Turn off non-essential notifications in the Settings menu.

- Disable notifications for shared calendars you don't actively use.

Examples of Effective Notification Management

- Scenario 1: Managing Work Deadlines

Set a 1-day email reminder for major project deadlines, followed by a 15-minute pop-up alert.

- Scenario 2: Preparing for Meetings

Use push notifications 30 minutes before meetings to gather materials or join virtual calls.

- Scenario 3: Personal Appointments

For personal events like doctor appointments, opt for a single push notification on your phone.

Managing your Google Calendar notification preferences is key to staying organized without feeling overwhelmed. By tailoring settings to your needs, you can ensure you're always prepared and focused on what matters most.

4.2 Creating Multiple Calendars

Managing a busy life often means juggling multiple responsibilities—work, personal commitments, family events, and even hobbies. Google Calendar allows you to create multiple calendars to separate and organize different aspects of your life, ensuring clarity and ease of use. In this section, we'll walk you through the process of creating multiple calendars and using them effectively to stay organized.

4.2.1 Setting Up Work, Personal, and Shared Calendars

One of the most powerful features of Google Calendar is the ability to create and manage distinct calendars for different purposes. By separating your work and personal schedules—or even creating shared calendars for collaborative use—you can better manage your time and avoid confusion.

Step 1: Access the Calendar Creation Feature

Open Google Calendar

Navigate to [Google Calendar](https://calendar.google.com) in your browser or app. Ensure you're signed into the correct Google account.

Locate the "Add Calendar" Option

On the left-hand sidebar, find the section labeled "My Calendars." Click the "+" (plus) icon next to it, and then select "Create new calendar" from the dropdown menu.

Step 2: Define Your New Calendar

Name Your Calendar

- Enter a descriptive and relevant name for the calendar. For example:

  - "Work Projects" for your job-related tasks.

  - "Family Events" for birthdays and holidays.

  - "Fitness Goals" for tracking your workouts.

Add a Description

Use the Description field to clarify the purpose of the calendar. For instance, "This calendar tracks my project deadlines and team meetings."

Select a Time Zone

Choose the appropriate time zone. If you frequently collaborate with others in different regions, ensure this matches the time zone you're operating in to avoid scheduling conflicts.

Save the Calendar

Click the "Create Calendar" button to finalize and save your new calendar. It will now appear under the "My Calendars" section.

Step 3: Customize Your Calendar

Once the calendar is created, you can customize its settings:

Change the Calendar Color

Assign a unique color to your new calendar for visual distinction. Simply click on the three-dot menu next to the calendar's name under "My Calendars" and select "Choose color."

Set Default Notifications

Configure default notifications for events in this calendar. Go to the calendar settings, navigate to "Event notifications," and set reminders like:

- 10 minutes before for meetings.

- 1 day before for deadlines.

Step 4: Using Work and Personal Calendars Effectively

Work Calendar

Your work calendar can help you organize meetings, deadlines, and tasks. Here are some tips:

- Block Time for Focused Work

Use events to allocate time for deep work. For example, create a recurring event titled "Morning Focus" from 9:00 AM to 11:00 AM.

- Integrate with Gmail

Automatically add events from Gmail (e.g., flight bookings or restaurant reservations) to your calendar for seamless scheduling.

Personal Calendar

Use your personal calendar for family activities, hobbies, and self-care. Tips include:

- Set Recurring Events for Routines

Create events for daily exercise or weekly family dinners.

- Add Holidays

Enable public holidays by subscribing to your country's holiday calendar in the "Browse calendars of interest" section.

Step 5: Creating Shared Calendars

Shared calendars are excellent for teamwork or family collaboration. Here's how to create one:

1. Go to Calendar Settings

Select the newly created calendar and click on "Settings and sharing."

2. Share with Specific People

Under the "Share with specific people" section, add the email addresses of those you want to share the calendar with.

3. Adjust Permissions

Decide what level of access each person has:

- See only free/busy: They can view your availability without seeing event details.

- Make changes to events: Allows them to edit and add events.

4. Send Invitations

Click "Send" to notify collaborators. They will receive an email invitation to join the calendar.

Examples of Shared Calendars

- Family Calendar: Coordinate school activities, family vacations, and household tasks.

- Team Calendar: Track deadlines, meetings, and project milestones.

Step 6: Sync and Organize Your Calendars

Sync Across Devices

Ensure your calendars are synced on all your devices by enabling sync in the Google Calendar app.

Overlay Multiple Calendars

View your calendars simultaneously by enabling overlays. This allows you to see work and personal schedules side-by-side, helping to avoid conflicts.

By setting up multiple calendars, you can declutter your schedule, maintain focus, and collaborate more effectively with others. The next section, "4.2.2 Managing Calendar Overlays," will explore how to visually organize and interact with multiple calendars in one unified view.

4.2.2 Managing Calendar Overlays

Google Calendar allows users to overlay multiple calendars in one unified view, making it easier to manage busy schedules without missing important events. This feature is particularly useful for individuals juggling various roles, such as work commitments, personal errands, and family activities. In this section, we'll explore the concept of calendar overlays, their benefits, and step-by-step instructions on how to use them effectively.

What Are Calendar Overlays?

Calendar overlays enable you to view multiple calendars simultaneously within a single interface. Instead of switching between individual calendars, you can layer them over each other to gain a consolidated perspective. Each calendar is typically assigned a unique color, making it easy to distinguish between different categories of events.

For example:

- A work calendar might use blue for meetings and deadlines.

- A personal calendar might be in green for appointments and hobbies.

- A shared family calendar might use red for events involving all family members.

By overlaying these calendars, you can quickly identify potential conflicts or gaps in your schedule.

Why Use Calendar Overlays?

- Enhanced Organization: Consolidate your schedules into a single view, reducing the likelihood of double-booking.

- Better Time Management: Quickly identify free time slots or overlapping commitments across various calendars.

- Collaboration Efficiency: When sharing calendars with others, overlays help you align schedules without constant back-and-forth communication.

- Customizable Visibility: You can toggle individual calendars on or off, depending on what's most relevant at the moment.

How to Manage Calendar Overlays

Step 1: Access the Calendar List

To begin managing calendar overlays:

1. Open Google Calendar in your web browser or mobile app.

2. Locate the calendar list on the left-hand sidebar (on desktop) or tap the menu icon (on mobile).

3. This list shows all the calendars linked to your account, including personal, work, shared, and subscribed calendars.

Step 2: Assign Colors to Calendars

Colors play a crucial role in making overlays visually effective. Assigning a unique color to each calendar helps you differentiate events at a glance:

1. Hover over a calendar in the list.

2. Click the three-dot menu (⋮) next to the calendar name.

3. Select a color from the palette or create a custom color.

4. Repeat this process for all calendars you frequently use.

Step 3: Enable or Disable Calendar Overlays

You may not always need to view all your calendars at once. Google Calendar lets you toggle individual calendars on or off:

1. Check or uncheck the box next to a calendar in the sidebar.

2. Checked calendars appear as overlays; unchecked calendars are hidden from view.

3. Use this feature to focus on specific aspects of your schedule when needed, such as work tasks during office hours.

Step 4: Adjust Calendar Order

If you have multiple calendars, you might want to arrange them for quick access:

1. Drag and drop calendars within the sidebar to reorder them.

2. Place frequently used calendars at the top for convenience.

Best Practices for Using Calendar Overlays

1. Keep Calendars Specific and Minimal

While it's tempting to create a calendar for every aspect of life, too many calendars can lead to clutter. Focus on creating calendars for major categories like work, personal life, and shared activities.

2. Use Consistent Color Coding

Maintain a consistent color scheme across calendars. For instance, always use shades of blue for work-related events, regardless of the calendar. This consistency reduces cognitive load when scanning your schedule.

3. Optimize Visibility Settings

If certain calendars are rarely used, consider hiding them from the main view. For example, long-term project calendars can remain unchecked until actively needed.

4. Share and Collaborate Wisely

When sharing calendars with others, ensure the permissions are appropriately set. Overlays work best when shared calendars have limited visibility to only relevant events.

5. Sync Across Devices

To ensure overlays function seamlessly, synchronize your Google Calendar across all your devices. This guarantees you're always viewing the most up-to-date version of your schedule.

Advanced Tips for Calendar Overlays

1. Layering Calendars with Subscriptions

Subscribe to public calendars (e.g., holidays, sports schedules, or academic timetables) to layer them with your personal events. Subscribed calendars can be toggled on or off depending on relevance.

2. Using Overlays for Team Collaboration

For work teams:

- Create separate calendars for each project.

- Overlay project calendars with your personal work calendar to ensure you're aware of critical milestones without overloading a single calendar.

3. Setting Calendar Priorities

Not all calendars are equal in importance. Highlight high-priority calendars by selecting bolder or brighter colors. This subtle visual cue can help you focus on key events.

4. Using Overlay Views for Conflict Resolution

When two or more events conflict, overlays make it easier to identify and address the issue. Use the drag-and-drop feature to reschedule events directly within the interface.

Troubleshooting Common Overlay Issues

1. Calendars Not Appearing in the Overlay

- Ensure the calendar is linked to your account.

- Check the visibility settings in the calendar list.

2. Overwhelmed by Too Many Overlays

- Reduce active calendars to only the most critical ones.

- Consider using filters or creating a custom calendar view.

3. Syncing Problems Across Devices

- Confirm you're signed into the same Google account on all devices.

- Refresh the calendar app or reinstall if necessary.

Conclusion

Mastering calendar overlays in Google Calendar can significantly enhance your ability to manage complex schedules. By thoughtfully assigning colors, toggling visibility, and leveraging advanced tips, you'll transform your Google Calendar into a powerful organizational tool. Take the time to customize your overlays today and enjoy seamless, stress-free scheduling!

4.3 Adding Calendars from Other Sources

Adding external calendars to your Google Calendar is a powerful way to centralize all your scheduling needs. Whether it's importing a colleague's work calendar, syncing public holiday schedules, or integrating other platforms, this feature allows you to stay informed without juggling multiple tools. In this section, we'll guide you through the various methods of adding calendars from other sources, along with tips to manage them effectively.

4.3.1 Importing Calendars via .ICS Files

One of the most common methods for adding external calendars is through .ICS files. These files are standard calendar file formats used across various platforms like Outlook, Apple Calendar, and more.

Step-by-Step Guide to Importing .ICS Files:

1. Obtain the .ICS File:

  - Export the calendar from the external platform.

  - Save the file to your computer.

  - Ensure the file is named clearly for easy identification.

2. Log into Google Calendar:

  - Open Google Calendar on your desktop browser.

  - Ensure you are signed into the correct Google account.

3. Import the File:

  - Click on the gear icon in the top-right corner and select Settings.

  - In the left-hand menu, choose Import & Export.

  - Under Import, click Select file from your computer.

  - Choose the .ICS file you saved earlier.

4. Choose a Destination Calendar:

  - Select the calendar where you want the events to appear (e.g., Personal, Work).

  - Click Import to complete the process.

Troubleshooting Tips:

- If events don't appear, verify that the file contains valid data.

- Ensure the file isn't corrupted or improperly formatted.

- Confirm that you're importing into the intended calendar.

4.3.2 Adding Public Calendars

Google Calendar allows you to subscribe to a wide variety of public calendars, such as national holidays, sports schedules, or even moon phases. These are pre-made calendars designed for easy integration.

How to Add Public Calendars:

1. Open Calendar Settings:

  - Navigate to Google Calendar in your browser.

  - Click the + icon next to Other Calendars on the left sidebar.

2. Browse for Public Calendars:

  - Select Browse calendars of interest from the menu.

  - Explore the available options, such as holidays, sports, or religious observances.

3. Subscribe to a Calendar:

  - Click the checkbox next to the calendar you wish to add.

  - The calendar will automatically appear in your list under Other Calendars.

Customization Options:

- Change the color of the subscribed calendar for better differentiation.

- Hide or show the calendar as needed by toggling its visibility.

4.3.3 Syncing Calendars from External Platforms

Many platforms, like Microsoft Outlook or Apple Calendar, allow real-time syncing with Google Calendar. This is useful for maintaining consistency across tools, especially for work and personal commitments.

How to Sync Calendars:

For Microsoft Outlook:

1. Export your Outlook calendar as an .ICS file or get a shareable link.

2. Use the Import method (see Section 4.3.1) for .ICS files, or:

   - If you have a shareable link, click + Add Other Calendars in Google Calendar.

   - Select From URL, paste the link, and click Add Calendar.

For Apple Calendar (iCloud):

1. In iCloud, navigate to Calendars and select the one you want to share.

2. Enable Public Calendar and copy the provided URL.

3. Add this URL to Google Calendar by selecting + Add Other Calendars > From URL.

For Third-Party Platforms:

1. Check if the platform offers Google Calendar integration or a sync option.

2. Follow the platform-specific instructions for connecting the two systems.

Note: Real-time updates depend on the syncing capabilities of the external platform.

4.3.4 Managing Imported and Synced Calendars

Once you've added external calendars, it's crucial to manage them effectively. Here are tips to keep your calendar organized:

Renaming and Reorganizing Calendars:

- Rename imported calendars for clarity.

   - In Settings, find the calendar under Settings for Other Calendars.

- Update the name field to something intuitive (e.g., "Work Meetings," "Sports Schedule").

Setting Notification Preferences:

- Avoid clutter by adjusting notifications for each calendar.

  - Turn off reminders for non-critical calendars like public holidays.

  - Customize alerts for synced work calendars to match your preferences.

Adjusting Calendar Permissions:

- Control who can view or edit your external calendars.

  - Use the Share Settings to limit or expand access as needed.

4.3.5 Common Challenges and Solutions

Issue: Events Not Showing Up

- Ensure the external calendar is enabled in Google Calendar's sidebar.

- Refresh your browser or app to sync the latest updates.

Issue: Duplicate Events

- This can occur if the same calendar is added multiple times.

- Check the Other Calendars list and remove duplicates.

Issue: Time Zone Conflicts

- Verify that the time zones of the external calendar and Google Calendar match.

- Adjust settings in Calendar Settings > Time Zone if discrepancies exist.

Adding calendars from other sources allows you to fully harness the flexibility and power of Google Calendar. By centralizing all your scheduling needs, you can streamline your planning process and stay on top of everything in one convenient location. With these tips, you're ready to take full advantage of external calendar integration.

CHAPTER V
Integrations and Automation

5.1 Connecting Google Calendar to Other Tools

Google Calendar is not just a standalone tool; its true power lies in its ability to seamlessly integrate with other applications, enabling a cohesive ecosystem for managing your time and tasks. Among the most useful integrations are Gmail and Google Meet, two essential components of the Google Workspace suite. By connecting Google Calendar with these tools, you can enhance your productivity and streamline your daily workflows.

5.1.1 Integrating with Gmail and Google Meet

Why Integrate Google Calendar with Gmail?

Gmail is at the heart of many people's digital communications. Whether you're receiving meeting invitations, task assignments, or event details, much of the information you need to schedule and manage your time already lives in your inbox. Integrating Gmail with Google Calendar simplifies the process of turning emails into actionable calendar items. Instead of copying and pasting event details or manually inputting times and dates, Gmail allows you to create events with just a few clicks, ensuring accuracy and saving time.

Setting Up the Integration

Integrating Gmail with Google Calendar is straightforward since they are both part of the Google ecosystem. Here's how you can leverage this integration:

1. Automatic Event Creation:

   - By default, Google Calendar can automatically create events from emails. For example, when you receive an email confirmation for a flight, hotel booking, or restaurant reservation, Gmail will recognize the details and add the event to your Google Calendar.

- To enable or adjust this feature:

  - Open Google Calendar.

  - Go to Settings > Events from Gmail.

  - Ensure the box for "Automatically add events from Gmail to my calendar" is checked.

  - Customize notification settings to ensure you are reminded of these events at the right time.

2. Adding Events Directly from Gmail:

 - When you receive an email with event details, such as a meeting invitation, you'll often see an "Add to Calendar" button in the email. Clicking this button will take you to Google Calendar, where you can confirm the event details and save it.

3. Attaching Emails to Calendar Events:

 - For context-rich events, you can attach the original email to the calendar entry. This ensures you have all the relevant details, such as meeting agendas or guest lists, in one place.

  - To do this:

   - Open the event in Google Calendar.

   - Select Add Description or Add Attachment, then locate the email link in your Google Drive.

Why Integrate Google Meet with Google Calendar?

Google Meet is a powerful video conferencing tool that enables seamless virtual collaboration. Integrating it with Google Calendar simplifies the process of scheduling, joining, and managing virtual meetings. Whenever you create an event in Google Calendar, you can easily add a Google Meet link, ensuring that participants can join with a single click.

Setting Up Google Meet Integration

1. Creating Events with Google Meet Links:

 - When scheduling an event in Google Calendar:

- Open Google Calendar and click the Create button.

- Add event details such as the title, date, and time.

- Under the location field, click Add Google Meet Video Conferencing. A unique Google Meet link will automatically be generated and included in the event.

2. Adding Google Meet Links to Existing Events:

- If you forget to include a Google Meet link while creating an event, you can always edit the event and add it later.

- Open the event, click Edit, and select the Add Google Meet Video Conferencing option.

3. Joining Google Meet Directly from Google Calendar:

- On the day of the meeting, you'll see the event on your calendar. Click the event to expand it, and select the Join with Google Meet button to be taken directly to the meeting.

4. Managing Participant Access:

- Google Calendar allows you to control who can join your meeting through invitation settings.

- When adding guests to the calendar event, you can choose whether they are required to sign in with a Google account or can join as a guest.

Advanced Features of Gmail and Google Meet Integration

1. Time Zone Adjustments:

- If participants are in different time zones, Google Calendar automatically adjusts the event time based on each user's settings. This ensures that everyone receives an invite tailored to their local time.

2. Meeting Preparation with Attached Documents:

- Google Calendar allows you to attach documents, slides, or spreadsheets to events. This feature is particularly useful for meetings scheduled through Google Meet. Attendees can review the materials ahead of time, leading to more productive discussions.

3. Email Follow-Ups:

- After a meeting, you can easily send follow-up emails from Gmail by referencing the calendar event. The seamless transition between tools ensures you don't miss out on post-meeting action items.

Practical Scenarios of Integration

1. Scheduling Team Meetings:

- Use Google Calendar to schedule recurring team check-ins and automatically generate Google Meet links for virtual attendees.

- Attach the meeting agenda, created in Google Docs, to the event for easy access.

2. Tracking Personal Appointments:

- When you receive a confirmation email for a doctor's appointment or a family gathering, Google Calendar ensures that these personal events don't conflict with your work schedule.

3. Streamlining Project Collaboration:

- For project-based work, schedule deadlines and brainstorming sessions in Google Calendar, include Google Meet links, and attach shared files directly from Gmail.

Tips for Maximizing the Integration

- *Leverage Keyboard Shortcuts:* Both Gmail and Google Calendar offer shortcuts that speed up the process of navigating between tools and creating events.

- *Enable Notifications Across Devices*: Ensure that you receive event reminders via both email and mobile notifications to stay on top of your schedule.

- *Regularly Review and Update Event Details*: Periodically check your calendar for automatically added events to ensure all details are correct and up-to-date.

By connecting Gmail and Google Meet with Google Calendar, you create a unified system that keeps your schedule organized, your communications streamlined, and your meetings hassle-free. The seamless integration between these tools saves time, reduces errors, and enhances overall productivity, making it an essential strategy for managing both personal and professional commitments.

5.1.2 Syncing with Third-Party Apps

One of the most powerful features of Google Calendar is its ability to sync seamlessly with a variety of third-party applications. This integration enhances your productivity, allowing you to centralize your schedules, streamline workflows, and avoid the pitfalls of missed appointments or double bookings. In this section, we'll explore the types of third-party apps that can be synced with Google Calendar, how to set up these integrations, and the practical benefits they bring to both personal and professional settings.

The Importance of Syncing with Third-Party Apps

In today's digital ecosystem, no single app can fulfill every need. You might use project management tools like Trello or Asana, communication platforms like Slack or Microsoft Teams, and fitness apps like Strava. By syncing these tools with Google Calendar, you ensure that your time is managed holistically. This integration eliminates redundancy, reduces manual input, and creates a single, cohesive view of your day-to-day activities.

Common Third-Party Apps to Sync with Google Calendar

1. **Project Management Tools**

    o **Trello**: Syncing Trello with Google Calendar lets you view card deadlines and board updates directly in your calendar. You can visualize tasks across projects alongside other commitments, enabling better time allocation.

    o **Asana**: Asana allows project tasks and milestones to appear in Google Calendar. This sync ensures that deadlines from your project management software are automatically reflected in your schedule.

2. **Communication Platforms**

    o **Slack**: Integrating Slack with Google Calendar enables automatic updates about meeting times and status changes. Slack notifications ensure you stay informed without toggling between apps.

- ○ **Microsoft Teams**: Syncing Teams with Google Calendar provides a unified view of scheduled meetings across platforms, reducing the risk of overlapping events.

3. **Fitness and Health Apps**

   - ○ **Strava**: For fitness enthusiasts, syncing Strava activities with Google Calendar keeps workout schedules and activity tracking organized in one place.

   - ○ **MyFitnessPal**: Integrating health apps allows you to monitor meal plans or fitness goals alongside work commitments, promoting a balanced lifestyle.

4. **Travel and Booking Services**

   - ○ **TripIt**: By syncing TripIt with Google Calendar, your travel itineraries, including flight times and hotel check-ins, are added automatically to your schedule.

   - ○ **OpenTable**: Dinner reservations from OpenTable can be synced, making it easier to plan social or professional gatherings without overlap.

5. **Task and Reminder Tools**

   - ○ **Todoist**: Syncing Todoist with Google Calendar ensures task deadlines and reminders are visually integrated into your day.

   - ○ **Evernote**: Use Evernote's calendar integration to link notes with corresponding events for easy access during meetings.

How to Sync Third-Party Apps with Google Calendar

Syncing third-party apps with Google Calendar is often straightforward, but the process may vary depending on the application. Below is a general guide for most integrations:

1. **Access the App Settings**
   Open the third-party app you wish to sync. Navigate to the settings menu and look for a "Calendar Sync" or "Integration" option.

2. **Authorize Google Calendar Access**
   Many apps will prompt you to log in to your Google account and grant permissions. Make sure you understand what data the app will access and share.

3. **Configure Sync Settings**
   Choose specific calendars (if applicable) or customize how data will appear in your Google Calendar. For example, you might want task deadlines to show but omit non-essential updates.

4. **Test the Integration**
   Once the setup is complete, test the integration by adding a task, event, or update in the third-party app. Verify that it appears correctly in Google Calendar.

Practical Benefits of Third-Party Syncing

1. **Centralized Scheduling**
   A single view of all events, tasks, and reminders saves you from juggling multiple tools. For instance, integrating Asana and Slack ensures your work commitments and team updates are consolidated in Google Calendar.

2. **Enhanced Collaboration**
   Syncing shared tools like Trello or Microsoft Teams with Google Calendar keeps everyone on the same page, reducing miscommunications. Team members can easily reference project timelines directly within their calendars.

3. **Improved Time Management**
   Seeing all activities in one place helps prioritize tasks effectively. If a task deadline overlaps with a meeting, you can reschedule proactively.

4. **Reduced Manual Entry**
   Automated syncing eliminates the need to manually input information into your calendar. This saves time and minimizes errors, especially when managing complex schedules.

Troubleshooting Sync Issues

While syncing Google Calendar with third-party apps is generally reliable, occasional issues may arise. Here are some common problems and solutions:

1. **Events Not Appearing**

   o   Check if the third-party app has the necessary permissions to access your Google Calendar.

   o   Ensure the sync settings are correctly configured in both applications.

2. **Duplicate Events**

   o   This issue often occurs if you have multiple sync integrations for the same app. Review and consolidate your settings to avoid duplication.

3. **Outdated Information**

   o   Syncing delays can sometimes cause outdated data to appear. Manually refresh the app or Google Calendar to update information.

4. **Connectivity Problems**

   o   Ensure a stable internet connection during the setup process. Some integrations require active connections for real-time updates.

Real-Life Examples of Third-Party Sync Success

1. **Freelancers and Remote Workers**
   Jane, a freelance graphic designer, uses Trello for project management and Google Calendar for her personal schedule. By syncing the two, she avoids double bookings, tracks client deadlines, and balances work-life priorities effectively.

2. **Fitness Enthusiasts**
   Mike, a marathon runner, syncs Strava with Google Calendar to plan his training runs around work meetings. This integration helps him stay consistent with his fitness goals without neglecting professional commitments.

3. **Small Business Owners**
   Sarah, a café owner, integrates OpenTable and Todoist with Google Calendar. This allows her to track reservations and daily tasks efficiently while focusing on growing her business.

Conclusion

Syncing Google Calendar with third-party apps is a game-changing way to optimize your productivity. By consolidating multiple tools into one centralized system, you gain better control over your schedule, improve collaboration, and achieve a seamless workflow. Whether you're managing personal tasks, professional projects, or fitness goals, these integrations unlock the full potential of Google Calendar as your ultimate planning hub.

5.2 Using Google Calendar with Smart Devices

Smart devices have revolutionized the way we interact with our calendars, making scheduling, reminders, and event management more accessible than ever. Google Calendar integrates seamlessly with a wide array of smart devices, allowing you to access and manage your schedule on the go, hands-free, and even in real-time. In this section, we will explore how to maximize your productivity by connecting Google Calendar to smart devices like smartphones, tablets, smart speakers, and wearables.

5.2.1 Voice Commands with Google Assistant

Voice commands, powered by Google Assistant, are among the most efficient tools for managing your Google Calendar. With just your voice, you can create events, set reminders, check your schedule, and even receive real-time updates. This hands-free approach is particularly useful for busy professionals, multitaskers, or anyone who wants to streamline their day.

Setting Up Google Assistant with Your Calendar

To start using Google Assistant for calendar management, you'll need to ensure that your devices are properly configured:

1. **Connect Your Google Account**:
   Make sure the Google account linked to your calendar is also connected to your Google Assistant. You can verify this in the Google Home app or the settings menu on your smartphone.

2. **Enable Calendar Permissions**:
   Grant Google Assistant access to your calendar data. This allows it to read your schedule, add events, and notify you about upcoming tasks.

3. **Activate Google Assistant on Your Devices**:
   Google Assistant is built into most Android devices and can be downloaded on iOS. Activate it with the wake phrase "Hey Google" or by pressing the dedicated Assistant button (if available).

4. **Check Compatibility**:
    Ensure your smart devices, such as speakers or smart displays, are compatible with Google Assistant. Popular options include Google Nest devices and smart speakers from third-party manufacturers.

Using Voice Commands to Manage Events

Once everything is set up, you can use simple voice commands to interact with Google Calendar. Here are some examples of what you can do:

1. Creating Events

Easily schedule events without typing:

- "Hey Google, create an event called 'Team Meeting' on Friday at 3 PM."

- "Add 'Doctor's Appointment' to my calendar for next Tuesday at 10 AM."

Google Assistant will confirm the details before adding the event to your calendar.

2. Checking Your Schedule

Quickly get an overview of your day or week:

- "Hey Google, what's on my calendar today?"

- "Do I have any events tomorrow?"

For specific timeframes, try:

- "What's on my schedule this weekend?"

- "Show me my meetings for next Monday."

3. Setting Reminders and Notifications

You can also use Google Assistant to set reminders for tasks:

- "Hey Google, remind me to call Sarah at 2 PM tomorrow."

- "Set a reminder for 'Submit report' at 5 PM today."

These reminders will sync with your calendar and other Google apps.

4. Modifying or Cancelling Events

You can update events with commands like:

- "Hey Google, change my lunch meeting to 1 PM."

- "Cancel my workout session for Thursday."

This feature is particularly helpful when plans change, allowing you to adjust on the fly.

Getting Creative with Voice Commands

Google Assistant goes beyond basic scheduling. Use these creative voice commands to make the most of your calendar:

1. **Add Notes or Locations**:
   Include additional details for better context:

   - "Hey Google, add '123 Main Street' as the location for my 3 PM meeting."

   - "Attach 'Client Report' to my event on Friday at 10 AM."

2. **Set Up Repeating Events**:
   Schedule recurring events without hassle:

   - "Hey Google, add 'Yoga Class' every Tuesday and Thursday at 6 PM."

   - "Create a repeating event for 'Weekly Check-In' every Monday at 9 AM."

3. **Plan Travel and Time Zones**:
   Google Assistant can help with events across time zones:

   - "Hey Google, add 'Conference Call with London' on Wednesday at 3 PM GMT."

   - "What time is my flight to New York tomorrow?"

4. **Daily Summaries**:
   Ask for a morning briefing to start your day:

   - "Hey Google, tell me about my day."

   - "What's my first meeting today?"

Benefits of Using Voice Commands

1. Hands-Free Convenience

Voice commands allow you to manage your calendar without touching a device. This is particularly useful while driving, cooking, or working on tasks that require your hands.

2. Real-Time Adjustments

With instant updates, you can quickly react to changes in your schedule, keeping everything up to date.

3. Improved Productivity

Eliminating the need to manually type or navigate through menus saves time and reduces distractions, helping you focus on more critical tasks.

4. Enhanced Accessibility

Voice commands make calendar management accessible for users with physical disabilities or those less familiar with traditional interfaces.

Troubleshooting Voice Commands

While Google Assistant is highly reliable, you may encounter occasional issues. Here's how to address them:

1. **Unrecognized Commands**:
   Ensure you're using the correct syntax. For example, be specific about dates, times, and event names.

2. **Connectivity Issues**:
   Verify that your device has a stable internet connection. Google Assistant requires online access to sync with your calendar.

3. **Sync Errors**:
   If events don't appear in your calendar, recheck your account permissions and ensure synchronization is enabled in the Google Calendar settings.

4. **Device Compatibility**:
   If your device doesn't respond, ensure it supports Google Assistant and that the app is up to date.

Future Possibilities with Google Assistant and Smart Devices

The integration between Google Calendar and smart devices continues to evolve. Features like AI-generated schedule recommendations, advanced voice recognition, and deeper integration with third-party apps are likely to make calendar management even more intuitive in the future.

By mastering voice commands with Google Assistant, you can transform your Google Calendar into a true productivity powerhouse. Whether you're juggling work, family, or personal commitments, these tools are designed to make life easier, one command at a time.

5.2.2 Smart Notifications on Mobile Devices

Smart notifications are one of the most powerful features of Google Calendar, enabling users to stay on top of their schedules while leveraging the convenience of mobile technology. In this section, we'll explore the types of notifications available, how to configure them for maximum efficiency, and best practices to ensure that you never miss a meeting or deadline.

Understanding Smart Notifications

Smart notifications are more than just simple reminders. They are designed to provide context-aware alerts based on your schedule and location. For example, Google Calendar can send you a notification to leave for an event based on real-time traffic conditions or remind you to prepare for a meeting with attached documents.

Key features of smart notifications include:

- **Event Reminders**: Notifications for upcoming events, tasks, or deadlines.

- **Travel Time Alerts**: Notifications to leave early based on traffic or transit conditions.

- **Customizable Notifications**: Options to set alerts based on your preferences, such as minutes, hours, or days before an event.

Configuring Smart Notifications

Setting up notifications on your mobile device ensures that you receive timely alerts wherever you are. Here's how you can configure them:

Step 1: Enable Notifications in Google Calendar App

1. Open the Google Calendar app on your mobile device.

2. Tap the menu icon (three horizontal lines) in the top-left corner.

3. Scroll down and select **Settings**.

4. Choose the calendar you want to customize notifications for.

5. Under **Notifications**, tap on **Event notifications** to add or edit alerts.

Step 2: Choose Notification Types

You can choose between two primary types of notifications:

- **Pop-up Notifications**: These appear directly on your device's screen, ensuring you don't miss them.

- **Email Notifications**: Useful for detailed reminders, especially for events requiring preparation.

Step 3: Customize Alert Times

You can set alerts to appear at specific intervals before an event. For example:

- 10 minutes before a meeting to gather materials.

- 1 hour before a flight to start heading to the airport.

Step 4: Enable Travel Notifications

To activate travel alerts:

1. Ensure your event includes a location.

2. Google Calendar will automatically calculate travel time and send notifications accordingly.

Leveraging Location-Based Alerts

One of the standout features of smart notifications is their ability to adapt based on your location. By enabling location services on your mobile device, Google Calendar can:

- Notify you to leave early if there's unexpected traffic.

- Suggest alternate routes if delays occur.

- Provide estimated travel times directly in the notification.

To enable location-based alerts:

1. Go to your device's settings and ensure location services are enabled for Google Calendar.

2. Add precise addresses to your events for accurate travel estimates.

Syncing Notifications Across Devices

With Google Calendar, your notifications can sync seamlessly across devices, ensuring you receive alerts on both your smartphone and other connected devices, like tablets or smartwatches.

Tips for Effective Syncing:

- **Enable Sync Across Devices**: In the app settings, ensure the calendar is synced.

- **Test Notifications**: Check that notifications appear on all intended devices.

- **Integrate with Wearables**: Pair your smartwatch to receive discreet notifications during meetings or while on the go.

Best Practices for Managing Notifications

While notifications are incredibly helpful, too many can become overwhelming. Here's how to make the most of them without feeling bombarded:

1. Prioritize Key Alerts

Not all events require notifications. Reserve alerts for high-priority tasks, appointments, or deadlines.

2. Use Multiple Notifications Wisely

For important events, set multiple reminders. For example:

- An alert 1 day before to prepare.

- Another alert 15 minutes before to ensure you're ready.

3. Adjust Quiet Hours

Avoid unnecessary distractions by enabling **Do Not Disturb** mode during specific times, such as late at night or during focus periods. Google Calendar allows you to customize notification settings to respect your quiet hours.

Troubleshooting Notification Issues

If you're not receiving notifications as expected, consider the following solutions:

Common Issues and Fixes

- **Notifications Not Appearing**: Check if notifications are enabled in both the app and device settings.

- **Battery Saver Mode Interference**: Some devices restrict notifications in battery-saving mode. Add Google Calendar as an exception.

- **App Not Updated**: Ensure you have the latest version of the Google Calendar app.

Examples of Smart Notification Usage

1. **Professional Scenario**: You have a client meeting at 10:00 AM in downtown. Google Calendar sends you a notification at 9:00 AM, advising you to leave early due to traffic congestion.

2. **Personal Scenario**: Your friend's birthday dinner is scheduled at 7:00 PM. A reminder pops up at 6:30 PM, and the event description includes the restaurant address and your RSVP.

3. **Multi-Device Scenario**: You receive a travel alert on your phone and a follow-up reminder on your smartwatch as you're about to leave the office.

Future Trends in Smart Notifications

Google Calendar continues to evolve, incorporating AI-driven insights to make notifications even smarter. Imagine notifications that:

- Automatically reschedule events based on unexpected conflicts.

- Offer proactive reminders to review documents before meetings.

- Provide weather alerts for outdoor events.

Conclusion

Smart notifications on mobile devices are an indispensable tool for anyone looking to streamline their daily life. By setting up and optimizing these features, you can ensure that you're always prepared, punctual, and in control of your schedule. Take the time to experiment with notification settings to find what works best for you, and let Google Calendar handle the rest.

5.3 Automating Tasks with Add-Ons and APIs

Automation is a powerful feature of Google Calendar that allows you to streamline workflows, reduce manual effort, and enhance productivity. By leveraging add-ons and Application Programming Interfaces (APIs), you can customize and expand Google Calendar's capabilities to fit your specific needs. This section delves into how you can use these tools to automate tasks, integrate with other platforms, and maximize your efficiency.

5.3.1 Understanding Add-Ons in Google Calendar

Add-ons are pre-built tools and extensions that integrate seamlessly with Google Calendar. They allow you to connect your calendar with third-party applications and enable new features without needing advanced technical skills.

Finding and Installing Add-Ons

1. **Accessing the Add-On Store:**
   Navigate to the Google Calendar interface and locate the gear icon (settings). From the drop-down menu, select "Get Add-ons." This will open the Google Workspace Marketplace, where you can explore various tools tailored for different needs.

2. **Popular Add-Ons for Automation:**

   o **Zoom and Microsoft Teams:** Automatically generate meeting links when scheduling events.

   o **Slack:** Sync your calendar to send reminders or display your availability in Slack channels.

   o **Trello:** Create Trello cards directly from events on your Google Calendar.

   o **Zapier:** Automate workflows by connecting Google Calendar with over 5,000 apps.

3. **Installing an Add-On:**
   Once you've selected an add-on, click "Install" and follow the prompts to grant necessary permissions. The add-on will then appear in your calendar interface, ready for use.

Using Add-Ons Effectively

To maximize the benefits of add-ons, focus on those that align with your daily tasks. For example:

- **For project managers**: Use add-ons that link project management tools like Asana or Monday.com to keep track of deadlines.

- **For remote workers**: Integrate conferencing apps to simplify meeting scheduling.

- **For personal productivity**: Employ task management add-ons such as Todoist for seamless tracking of to-do lists.

5.3.2 Exploring Google Calendar APIs for Developers

For those with technical expertise, Google Calendar's APIs open the door to advanced customization. APIs enable you to build unique applications, integrate Google Calendar into existing software, or automate complex workflows.

Getting Started with the Google Calendar API

1. **Understanding the Basics**:
   The Google Calendar API allows developers to interact programmatically with Google Calendar. It uses RESTful endpoints to perform actions like creating events, retrieving calendar data, and updating event details.

2. **Setting Up API Access**:
   - Go to the Google Cloud Console and create a new project.
   - Enable the Google Calendar API for the project.
   - Generate API credentials, such as an API key or OAuth 2.0 client credentials, depending on your application's requirements.

3. **Exploring API Capabilities**:
   - **Event Management**: Programmatically add, update, or delete events.
   - **Calendar Customization**: Create and manage multiple calendars for different purposes.

- o **Data Retrieval**: Access event details, participant information, and calendar summaries.

Building Automation with APIs

Here are some practical examples of how APIs can streamline workflows:

- **Automated Scheduling**: Develop an app that schedules meetings by finding mutually available time slots for all participants.

- **Custom Notifications**: Set up personalized reminders via email or SMS when events are added or modified.

- **Integration with CRM Systems**: Sync customer meetings from a CRM tool directly into Google Calendar.

Using Client Libraries for Simplified Coding

Google provides client libraries in multiple programming languages (Python, Java, JavaScript, etc.) to simplify API usage. These libraries handle authentication and API calls, allowing you to focus on building features.

5.3.3 Advanced Automation Scenarios

Combining add-ons and APIs allows for powerful automation setups. Here are some scenarios to inspire your use of these tools:

1. Automating Meeting Workflows

- Use a tool like Zapier to automate meeting preparation. For instance, when a new meeting is scheduled, a Zap can:

  - o Send participants an agenda via email.

  - o Create a Google Drive folder for shared documents.

  - o Add meeting notes to a project management app.

2. Dynamic Task Assignment

- Build an API-based application that creates calendar events based on project milestones. When a project phase is completed in a task tracker, the app schedules a review meeting or deadline reminder.

3. Real-Time Notifications

- Integrate APIs with messaging apps like Slack or Microsoft Teams to send real-time updates about changes to important events.

4. Event Analytics

- Use APIs to pull event data into a dashboard for analyzing time spent in meetings, identifying patterns, or optimizing scheduling.

5.3.4 Tips for Successful Automation

1. **Start Small**: Focus on automating repetitive tasks that consume the most time, then gradually expand your setup.

2. **Test Thoroughly**: Ensure your add-ons or custom API scripts work as intended and don't conflict with existing workflows.

3. **Prioritize Security**: Always use secure authentication methods (like OAuth 2.0) and follow best practices for handling sensitive data.

4. **Keep it Updated**: Regularly review and update your automations to align with changes in your workflows or business needs.

5. **Leverage Community Support**: Explore forums, developer communities, and the Google Workspace Marketplace for inspiration and troubleshooting.

Conclusion

Automating tasks with add-ons and APIs transforms Google Calendar from a basic scheduling tool into a dynamic hub for productivity. Whether you use pre-built add-ons or develop custom solutions with APIs, these tools empower you to save time, reduce errors, and focus on what matters most. By embracing these technologies, you'll unlock the full potential of Google Calendar as your personal or professional assistant.

CHAPTER VI
Tips and Tricks for Efficiency

6.1 Keyboard Shortcuts

Google Calendar is a tool designed for efficiency, and learning its keyboard shortcuts can elevate your productivity to a whole new level. With these shortcuts, you can navigate, create events, and manage your calendar quickly without relying on a mouse or touchpad. This chapter introduces the essential keyboard shortcuts for Google Calendar, categorizes them by function, and offers practical tips on incorporating them into your daily routine.

6.1.1 Why Use Keyboard Shortcuts?

Keyboard shortcuts aren't just for tech enthusiasts; they are practical tools that save time and effort. Here are the primary benefits:

- **Speed:** Quickly perform actions like creating events, switching views, or searching your calendar.

- **Efficiency:** Reduce reliance on menus and clicks, making the user experience seamless.

- **Accessibility:** Keyboard shortcuts are especially useful for users with mobility challenges or for those using laptops with smaller trackpads.

6.1.2 Essential Google Calendar Keyboard Shortcuts

Below are the most important keyboard shortcuts you'll want to learn. These are organized into categories for ease of use.

Navigating the Calendar

- **t:** Jump to today's date.

- **g:** Go to a specific date. A dialog box appears where you can type in the desired date.

- **d, w, m:** Switch views:

    o   d for Day view.

    o   w for Week view.

    o   m for Month view.

- **x:** Switch to custom view (e.g., 4 days if your settings specify this).

- **a:** Switch to Schedule view, which lists your upcoming events.

- **j, k:** Move forward (j) or backward (k) through time.

Creating and Managing Events

- **c:** Create a new event. This shortcut opens the event creation window immediately.

- **e:** Edit an event after selecting it.

- **Delete key:** Delete the selected event.

- **Ctrl (or Cmd) + Enter:** Save an event you're editing.

General Actions

- **q:** Open Quick Add to create events with natural language (e.g., "Meeting tomorrow at 3 PM").

- **/ (slash):** Focus the search bar to quickly find events or calendars.

- **Esc:** Close any open dialog box or cancel an action.

6.1.3 Advanced Shortcuts for Power Users

If you've mastered the basics, these advanced shortcuts will help you get even more out of Google Calendar:

Calendar Management

- **Ctrl (or Cmd) + Click:** Select multiple events or calendars to view them simultaneously.

- **Shift + Click:** Toggle visibility of a specific calendar in the sidebar.

Time Adjustments

- **Alt + Up/Down Arrow:** Adjust the event time in 15-minute increments when editing an event.

- **Alt + Left/Right Arrow:** Change the event date forward or backward by one day.

Accessing Calendar Settings

- **? (Shift + /):** Open the list of available keyboard shortcuts.

- **Alt + s:** Open Google Calendar settings in a new tab.

6.1.4 How to Memorize Keyboard Shortcuts

Learning shortcuts can feel overwhelming initially, but with consistent practice, they become second nature. Here are a few strategies:

1. **Start Small:** Focus on 2-3 shortcuts each week. For example, begin with c (create event), t (today), and / (search).

2. **Create a Reference Sheet:** Print a list of shortcuts and keep it near your workspace for quick reference.

3. **Use Them Daily:** Actively incorporate shortcuts into your daily routine. For instance, instead of clicking to navigate, use j or k to move through dates.

4. **Practice with Purpose:** Spend 5-10 minutes experimenting with shortcuts in Google Calendar, setting up mock events or switching views to reinforce muscle memory.

6.1.5 Troubleshooting Keyboard Shortcuts

Even the most well-designed shortcuts can sometimes fail. Below are common issues and solutions:

Issue 1: Shortcuts Aren't Working

- **Solution:** Ensure that keyboard shortcuts are enabled in your Google Calendar settings. Go to **Settings > Keyboard Shortcuts** and toggle the feature on.

Issue 2: Conflicts with Browser Extensions

- **Solution:** Some extensions may override Google Calendar shortcuts. Temporarily disable extensions or check their settings to resolve conflicts.

Issue 3: Different Operating Systems

- **Solution:** If you're using a Mac, remember to use the Cmd key instead of Ctrl for most shortcuts.

6.1.6 Maximizing Productivity with Shortcuts

To make the most of keyboard shortcuts:

- **Combine Shortcuts:** For instance, press / to search for an event, then use Enter to open it immediately, and e to edit.

- **Customize Your Workflow:** Tailor your use of shortcuts based on your scheduling needs. For example, if you frequently create events, prioritize learning the c and Ctrl + Enter combination.

- **Leverage Cross-App Shortcuts:** Use Google Calendar in tandem with Gmail or Google Docs, relying on shared shortcuts like / for search or Ctrl + Enter to save actions.

6.1.7 The Future of Keyboard Shortcuts

Google Calendar continues to evolve, and shortcuts may expand or change over time. Staying updated with new features will ensure that you remain a power user. Regularly check Google's official documentation or the **? (Shift + /)** shortcut for the latest additions.

By incorporating keyboard shortcuts into your workflow, you'll not only save time but also enjoy a more streamlined and enjoyable scheduling experience. Practice consistently, and watch as your productivity soars!

6.2 Hidden Features You Should Know

6.2.1 Event Attachments and Meeting Notes

Google Calendar is more than just a tool for scheduling; it's a platform that integrates seamlessly with your workflow, making it easier to manage meetings, share information, and keep track of important documents. One of its most underutilized features is the ability to attach files and notes to your events. These tools can save you time, enhance collaboration, and ensure that you have everything you need at your fingertips when the event begins.

What Are Event Attachments?

Event attachments are files that you can link directly to your calendar events. These could include documents, presentations, spreadsheets, images, or any other file stored in your Google Drive. By attaching these files, you ensure that all attendees have access to relevant materials before, during, and after the event.

This feature is especially helpful for:

- **Team meetings** where you need to review a specific document or presentation.

- **Client appointments** requiring prepared materials like proposals or contracts.

- **Workshops and training sessions** where attendees need handouts or pre-reading.

Benefits of Using Event Attachments

1. **Improved Organization:**
   Having all necessary documents linked directly to the event eliminates the need to dig through emails or cloud folders minutes before a meeting. Everything you need is just one click away.

2. **Enhanced Collaboration:**
   When you share an event attachment, all participants can view or edit it (depending on permissions). This ensures that everyone is on the same page and allows for real-time collaboration.

3. **Time-Saving:**
   Instead of sending separate emails with files, you can consolidate all your resources within the event itself.

4. **Error Reduction:**
   Sharing the wrong version of a document is a common mistake. Google Calendar ensures that everyone accesses the most up-to-date file stored in Google Drive.

How to Attach Files to an Event

Adding an attachment is straightforward:

1. **Create or Edit an Event:**
   Open Google Calendar and either create a new event or edit an existing one.

2. **Find the "Add Attachment" Option:**
   In the event details window, look for the paperclip icon labeled **"Add Attachment."** Click it to proceed.

3. **Select Your File:**
   A window will appear showing your Google Drive. Choose a file from your Drive or upload one directly from your computer.

4. **Grant Permissions:**
   Google Calendar will prompt you to adjust file permissions. Ensure that attendees have the necessary access, whether it's **view only**, **comment**, or **edit.**

5. **Save and Share:**
   Once the file is attached, save the event. The file will now appear in the event details, accessible to all invited participants.

Common Use Cases for Event Attachments

1. **Preparing for Business Meetings:**
   Imagine a weekly strategy session where your team reviews performance metrics. By attaching the latest report or slides to the event, you ensure everyone comes prepared.

2. **Client Deliverables:**
   If you're presenting a proposal to a client, attach the finalized version to the calendar event. This creates a centralized point for all materials.

3. **Educational Sessions:**
   For teachers or trainers, pre-reading materials or worksheets can be attached to the session, reducing the need for additional communication.

Meeting Notes in Google Calendar

Another invaluable feature is the integration of **Google Docs** for meeting notes. After creating an event, you can add collaborative notes to streamline discussions and document decisions in real time.

How to Add Meeting Notes:

1. Open your event in Google Calendar.

2. Click the **"Add Notes"** or **"Take Meeting Notes"** option.

3. A Google Doc template will be created and linked to the event.

Benefits of Meeting Notes Integration

1. **Real-Time Collaboration:**
   All participants can add comments, make edits, or highlight action items directly in the shared document during the meeting.

2. **Centralized Record Keeping:**
   After the meeting, the notes remain accessible in the event details, ensuring that nothing gets lost or overlooked.

3. **Ease of Follow-Up:**
   Use the notes to assign tasks or summarize decisions.

Tips for Maximizing Event Attachments and Notes

1. **Standardize Your Practices:**
   Create a routine for adding attachments and notes to events. For example, always link the agenda to meeting invites or upload reports the day before.

2. **Leverage Google Drive Integration:**
   Organize your Drive folders to align with your calendar structure. For instance, have a dedicated folder for each recurring meeting series.

3. **Assign a Note-Taker:**
   Designate one person to take notes during meetings. This ensures consistency and completeness.

4. **Review Permissions Regularly:**
   Before the meeting, double-check that all attendees have access to the attached files. This avoids delays during the session.

Potential Pitfalls and How to Avoid Them

1. **File Permissions Issues:**
   If attendees can't access a file, it disrupts the meeting. Always double-check permissions after adding an attachment.

2. **Overloading Events:**
   Adding too many attachments or irrelevant documents can clutter the event details. Be selective and only include essential materials.

3. **Neglecting to Update Files:**
   Ensure that the attached files are the latest versions. If you make changes after attaching a document, re-upload it to avoid confusion.

Conclusion

Mastering event attachments and meeting notes in Google Calendar can revolutionize how you plan and execute meetings. By consolidating materials and centralizing collaboration, you'll save time, reduce stress, and enhance productivity. As you incorporate these features into your routine, you'll discover new ways to streamline your schedule and make the most of Google Calendar's powerful tools.

6.2.2 Adding Public Holidays and Sports Schedules

Google Calendar is a powerful tool for managing your schedule, but one of its most underrated features is the ability to overlay external calendars, such as public holidays or sports schedules, directly into your main calendar view. This functionality not only simplifies planning around important dates but also ensures you never miss significant events that might impact your work or personal life. Here's how to unlock the full potential of this feature.

Why Add Public Holidays and Sports Schedules?

1. Better Planning Around Holidays

Public holidays vary depending on your country, state, or region. By adding these to your calendar, you can avoid scheduling conflicts, such as booking meetings or appointments on days when most people are unavailable. This feature is especially valuable for professionals working with international teams, as it helps accommodate diverse holiday schedules.

2. Stay Updated with Sports Events

If you're a sports enthusiast, adding game schedules of your favorite teams directly into your calendar ensures you never miss a match. This feature is also useful for parents with children in sports or for planning activities around major tournaments, such as the Olympics, FIFA World Cup, or the Super Bowl.

How to Add Public Holidays

Google Calendar makes it easy to integrate public holidays relevant to your location. Follow these steps:

Step 1: Open Google Calendar Settings

1. Navigate to your Google Calendar.

2. Click the gear icon in the top-right corner to access settings.

Step 2: Access the "Browse Calendars of Interest" Option

1. In the settings menu, locate the "Add calendar" section in the left-hand panel.

2. Click "Browse calendars of interest."

Step 3: Select Your Country or Region

1. Under the "Holidays" section, browse the list of available countries.

2. Select the calendar for your country to automatically add public holidays.

Step 4: View Holidays in Your Calendar

1. Once added, holidays will appear as all-day events in your calendar.

2. You can customize the color of the holiday calendar to differentiate it from other events.

How to Add Sports Schedules

If you're a fan of specific sports or teams, Google Calendar provides a straightforward way to integrate their schedules:

Step 1: Open the "Browse Calendars of Interest" Menu

1. Go to your calendar settings and navigate to the "Add calendar" section.

2. Select "Browse calendars of interest."

Step 2: Explore the Sports Section

1. Scroll to the "Sports" category.

2. Use the dropdown menus to select a sport, league, and specific team.

Step 3: Add the Team's Calendar

1. Click on the team you want to follow, and their schedule will automatically sync to your Google Calendar.

2. Each game will appear as an event, with details such as opponent, location, and start time.

Step 4: Stay Updated

Schedules are updated automatically, so you'll always have the latest information, including game postponements or rescheduling.

Customizing Public Holidays and Sports Schedules

Once these calendars are added, you can customize their appearance and functionality:

1. Adjusting Visibility

1. Use the checkboxes in the left-hand panel to toggle visibility for holiday or sports schedules.

2. This allows you to focus on specific events without overwhelming your main calendar view.

2. Setting Custom Colors

1. Assign unique colors to distinguish holidays or sports events from other calendar entries.

2. For example, you might choose green for holidays and blue for sports.

3. Creating Notifications

1. Add reminders for specific events, such as public holidays that may require advanced planning.

2. For sports fans, set alerts to ensure you tune in on time for the game.

Use Cases for Adding Public Holidays and Sports Schedules

1. Professional Use

- Team Collaboration: International companies can align project timelines with global holidays, avoiding delays caused by unplanned absences.

- Client Meetings: Sales professionals can schedule meetings with international clients more effectively by recognizing their local holidays.

2. Personal Use

- Vacation Planning: Integrate holidays into your calendar to optimize vacation schedules and take advantage of long weekends.

- Family Coordination: Plan family events around holidays and sports games, ensuring everyone is available.

3. Sports Enthusiasts

- Watch Parties: Plan gatherings with friends and family for big games by setting up reminders.

- Ticket Purchases: Stay informed about game dates to purchase tickets in advance.

Benefits of Integrating External Calendars

1. Time Efficiency

By having everything in one place, you save time switching between platforms or searching for schedules online.

2. Improved Organization

Overlaying external calendars helps you visualize your commitments and plan effectively around important events.

3. Seamless Synchronization

Changes to public holiday schedules or sports events are automatically updated, ensuring you're always working with the latest information.

Troubleshooting Common Issues

Even though adding public holidays and sports schedules is straightforward, occasional issues may arise:

1. Holidays Not Showing Up

- Ensure the correct country or region is selected.

- Check that the holiday calendar is enabled in the left-hand panel.

2. Duplicate Entries

- Avoid adding the same holiday or sports calendar multiple times to prevent duplicates.

- Review your settings and remove any unnecessary calendars.

3. Outdated Information

- While Google Calendar updates most schedules automatically, occasionally verify major events, especially for sports with frequent changes.

Maximizing the Feature

To fully benefit from this feature, consider integrating other related tools:

- Weather Forecasts: Add weather data alongside holiday and sports schedules for comprehensive planning.

- Third-Party Sports Apps: Sync detailed team statistics and updates using apps that integrate with Google Calendar.

Adding public holidays and sports schedules to your Google Calendar is more than a convenience—it's a game-changer for efficient planning. Whether you're balancing work, leisure, or both, this feature ensures you're always in the loop and ready to tackle your day with confidence.

6.3 Troubleshooting Common Issues

6.3.1 Syncing Errors

Syncing errors in Google Calendar can disrupt your schedule and create unnecessary confusion. Whether you're experiencing issues with events not appearing across devices or calendar updates not syncing correctly, these problems are both common and solvable. This section dives into the common causes of syncing errors, steps to diagnose the problem, and actionable solutions to resolve them.

Common Causes of Syncing Errors

1. **Connectivity Issues**

   o Google Calendar relies on an active internet connection to sync data. Poor or unstable connections can cause delays in syncing updates. If you're on a mobile device, switching between Wi-Fi and mobile data could also cause temporary syncing disruptions.

2. **Outdated Applications**

   o An outdated Google Calendar app or operating system might be incompatible with the latest sync protocols. Updates often include fixes for known issues and ensure compatibility across devices.

3. **Storage and Memory Constraints**

   o Devices with limited storage or running low on RAM might struggle to sync properly. Syncing requires background processes to run smoothly, and insufficient resources can cause delays or failures.

4. **Account Configuration Issues**

   o Syncing errors can occur if you've accidentally disabled synchronization for your Google account or the calendar app. Misconfigured settings can lead to specific calendars not syncing correctly.

5. **Conflicts with Other Applications**

   o Third-party apps or plugins interacting with Google Calendar can sometimes cause syncing conflicts. For instance, apps that modify or manage calendar data may inadvertently block or delay updates.

Steps to Diagnose Syncing Issues

1. **Check Your Internet Connection**

   o Ensure your device is connected to a stable and reliable internet connection. If you're on Wi-Fi, try running a speed test or switching to a different network. If you're using mobile data, confirm that your data plan is active and functioning.

2. **Verify Account Settings**

   o Open your Google Calendar app or access it via a browser. Ensure the correct Google account is linked and that syncing is enabled. On mobile devices, this can be found under *Settings > Accounts > Google*.

3. **Test Syncing Across Devices**

   o Create a test event on one device and check if it appears on another. If the event doesn't sync, the issue is likely device-specific. If it syncs on one device but not another, focus troubleshooting efforts on the problematic device.

4. **Review App Permissions**

   o Ensure that the Google Calendar app has the necessary permissions to access the internet, run in the background, and access calendar data. On mobile devices, this is usually under *Settings > Apps > Google Calendar > Permissions*.

5. **Check System Notifications**

   o Sometimes, Google sends alerts about account or sync issues. Check for notifications in the Google Calendar app or your Gmail account for any system messages.

Solutions to Resolve Syncing Errors

1. **Update the Google Calendar App**

   o Ensure you're using the latest version of the app. Updates often address bugs and improve syncing functionality. Visit the App Store or Google Play Store to download updates.

2. **Clear Cache and Data**

   o Cached data can become corrupted over time and disrupt syncing.

      ▪ On   Android: *Settings > Apps > Google Calendar > Storage > Clear Cache and Clear Data.*

      ▪ On iOS: Reinstalling the app is the quickest way to clear cache and data.

   o After clearing data, re-login to your account and check if syncing resumes.

3. **Resync Your Calendar**

   o Manually force Google Calendar to resync by disabling and re-enabling the sync option:

      ▪ *Settings > Accounts > Google > Sync Calendar* (toggle off and then on again).

   o On the web version, refresh the browser and ensure all connected calendars are selected for viewing.

4. **Free Up Storage and Memory**

   o Delete unnecessary files, apps, or data to free up resources on your device. For low-RAM devices, closing background apps can help improve syncing.

5. **Reinstall the App**

o Uninstalling and reinstalling the Google Calendar app can resolve deep-rooted issues. This process resets the app to its default state and prompts a full resync with your account.

6. **Check Server Status**

o Rarely, Google's servers may experience outages or maintenance. Visit the Google Workspace Status Dashboard to confirm if there are any ongoing issues.

7. **Review Calendar-Specific Settings**

o If a particular calendar isn't syncing:

▪ Go to *Settings > Manage Calendars* in the app and ensure the problematic calendar is enabled.

▪ Check that the calendar isn't hidden in the web version under *Settings > My Calendars > Show in List.*

8. **Remove and Re-add Your Account**

o Removing your Google account and re-adding it can refresh the syncing process:

▪ *Settings > Accounts > Google > Remove Account.*

▪ Re-add your account and ensure sync settings are enabled.

Preventing Future Syncing Issues

1. **Enable Automatic Updates**

o Set your device to update apps and the operating system automatically. This ensures compatibility and minimizes the risk of errors.

2. **Regularly Clear Cache**

o Periodically clear the cache to prevent data corruption. You can schedule this as part of your device's maintenance routine.

3. **Backup Calendar Data**

   o Export a copy of your calendar data periodically. This ensures you can recover important events in case of sync failures.

4. **Monitor App Permissions**

   o If you install new apps that interact with Google Calendar, review their permissions to ensure they don't interfere with syncing.

5. **Stay Informed**

   o Follow Google's updates and announcements regarding Calendar. Google occasionally introduces new features or fixes that may require user action.

When to Contact Support

If you've tried all troubleshooting steps and syncing errors persist, it may be time to contact Google support. Provide detailed information about the issue, including:

- Device type and operating system.

- Google Calendar app version.

- Steps you've already tried.

- Specific errors or behaviors observed.

Google offers support through the app, online help center, or their customer service channels.

By understanding and addressing syncing errors, you can ensure your Google Calendar remains a reliable tool for managing your schedule. Regular maintenance, attention to updates, and proactive troubleshooting will keep your calendar functioning seamlessly.

6.3.2 Resolving Overlapping Events

Managing overlapping events in Google Calendar is an essential skill for maintaining an organized and efficient schedule. Overlapping events can arise when multiple commitments coincide, leading to confusion or missed responsibilities. This section delves into strategies and tools available in Google Calendar to identify, manage, and resolve overlapping events effectively.

Understanding Overlapping Events

Overlapping events occur when two or more events are scheduled for the same time or when their durations overlap. For example:

- Scheduling a meeting at 10:00 AM while already having a doctor's appointment at the same time.

- Extending an event's duration into the time frame of another scheduled task.

Such conflicts can disrupt your workflow and potentially harm your credibility if commitments are missed.

Step 1: Identifying Overlapping Events

The first step to resolving overlapping events is identifying them. Google Calendar offers several features to help you spot scheduling conflicts:

1. **Visual Indicators:**
   Overlapping events are visually apparent on the calendar interface. Events in the same time block will either stack vertically or horizontally, depending on your view mode (Day, Week, or Month).

2. **Notifications:**
   If you're adding a new event that conflicts with an existing one, Google Calendar often prompts you with a warning about the overlap.

3. **Calendar Layers:**
   If you use multiple calendars (e.g., work, personal, or shared calendars), enable all relevant layers to view overlapping schedules.

Step 2: Assessing Priority and Flexibility

Not all overlapping events require immediate resolution. Evaluate each event to determine which takes precedence:

1. **Priority Analysis:**

   o **High Priority Events:** Non-negotiable commitments, such as a job interview or client meeting.

   o **Low Priority Events:** Tasks that can be rescheduled, like casual meetups or personal errands.

2. **Flexibility of Events:**
   Determine which events are more flexible. For instance, a recurring gym session might be easier to shift than a one-time workshop.

Step 3: Strategies for Resolving Overlaps

Once you've identified and assessed overlapping events, employ one or more of the following strategies to resolve the conflicts:

1. **Reschedule One or More Events:**

   o **Drag and Drop:** In Week or Day view, drag an event to a new time slot.

   o **Edit Event Details:** Open the event, adjust the time, and save changes.

2. **Shorten Event Durations:**
   If both events are necessary but time is limited, consider reducing their durations. For example, shorten a 1-hour meeting to 30 minutes.

3. **Combine Related Events:**
   If overlapping events are related, combine them into a single meeting or session. For instance, merge a brainstorming session with a project update meeting.

CHAPTER VI: TIPS AND TRICKS FOR EFFICIENCY

4. **Delegate or Decline Participation:**
    For events that require your presence but aren't critical, consider delegating to a colleague or declining with advance notice.

5. **Use Appointment Slots:**
    If you frequently host overlapping meetings, use Google Calendar's appointment slots to allocate specific times for others to book with you, avoiding conflicts.

Step 4: Automating Conflict Detection

Google Calendar provides automation tools to reduce the chances of overlaps:

1. **Enable Notifications for Conflicts:**
    In your settings, activate notifications for event conflicts. This ensures you'll receive alerts when new events overlap with existing ones.

2. **Set Working Hours:**
    Define your working hours in Google Calendar. Invites or events scheduled outside these hours will prompt participants to reschedule or choose alternate slots.

3. **Use Time Insights:**
    Time Insights (available in some Google Workspace plans) allows you to monitor how your time is allocated, helping identify patterns that lead to conflicts.

Step 5: Preventing Future Overlaps

Preventive measures can help you avoid overlapping events in the first place:

1. **Plan Ahead:**
    Regularly review your calendar to ensure adequate spacing between commitments.

2. **Buffer Time:**
    Schedule buffer time between events to account for travel, preparation, or unexpected delays.

3. **Synchronize All Calendars:**
   Integrate personal, work, and shared calendars into a unified view to minimize the risk of scheduling conflicts.

4. **Communicate Availability:**
   Share your calendar or mark busy slots to inform collaborators about your availability.

Case Study: Resolving a Real-Life Conflict

Scenario:
A marketing manager, Lisa, notices two overlapping events on her calendar: a client presentation at 11:00 AM and a team lunch scheduled from 10:30 AM to 12:00 PM.

Resolution:

1. Lisa prioritizes the client presentation, recognizing it as a high-stakes event.

2. She shortens the team lunch duration, moving it to 12:00 PM.

3. Lisa communicates the change to her team using the event update notification feature in Google Calendar.

4. She enables appointment slots for future team meetings to prevent similar overlaps.

Leveraging Google Calendar Features for Overlap Management

Google Calendar includes several tools that simplify overlap management:

1. **Find a Time:**
   For shared events, use the "Find a Time" feature to identify a time slot that works for all participants.

2. **Propose a New Time:**
   If invited to an event that conflicts with your schedule, propose a new time directly through the invitation interface.

3. **Color-Coding:**
   Use distinct colors for different types of events (e.g., personal, work, or shared) to easily spot potential overlaps.

Final Thoughts

Resolving overlapping events is crucial for maintaining a balanced and efficient schedule. With Google Calendar's robust features and proactive planning strategies, you can effectively manage conflicts, reduce stress, and focus on what truly matters. Regularly reviewing your calendar, prioritizing commitments, and leveraging available tools will ensure you stay on top of your schedule without compromising productivity.

CHAPTER VII
Managing Work-Life Balance

7.1 Using Google Calendar for Time Blocking

Time blocking is a powerful time management strategy that helps you take control of your schedule by dividing your day into focused blocks of time. By allocating specific time slots for tasks, meetings, and even relaxation, you can achieve better productivity, reduce decision fatigue, and maintain a healthy work-life balance. Google Calendar is an excellent tool to implement time blocking effectively. This section will guide you through the process, offering practical tips and insights for maximizing your efficiency.

What is Time Blocking?

Time blocking is a scheduling technique that involves assigning specific time periods to individual tasks or activities. Unlike traditional to-do lists, where tasks are often vague and unscheduled, time blocking ensures that every task has a designated time on your calendar.

Key benefits of time blocking include:

- **Increased Focus:** Helps you concentrate on one task at a time without distractions.
- **Better Time Management:** Provides a realistic view of how much you can accomplish in a day.
- **Improved Accountability:** Encourages you to stick to your planned schedule.
- **Reduced Stress:** Allows you to allocate time for both work and personal activities, ensuring balance.

Setting Up Your Calendar for Time Blocking

Before diving into time blocking, take a few preparatory steps to make your Google Calendar more effective:

1. **Create Separate Calendars for Different Areas of Life**
   Google Calendar allows you to create multiple calendars, which can be color-coded for easy identification. For example:

   o **Work:** Tasks, meetings, and deadlines.

   o **Personal:** Family events, hobbies, and fitness routines.

   o **Self-Care:** Downtime, relaxation, and mental health activities.

By organizing your schedule this way, you can view or hide specific calendars to focus on certain areas when needed.

2. **Define Your Priorities**
   Take some time to list out your most important tasks and commitments. Use these priorities to create blocks for:

   o High-priority tasks requiring deep focus.

   o Routine activities like checking emails or attending daily stand-up meetings.

   o Non-negotiable commitments, such as personal time or family obligations.

3. **Set Working Hours in Google Calendar**
   Define your working hours in the Calendar settings to prevent overbooking or scheduling conflicts outside your availability.

Creating Time Blocks

Here's how to use Google Calendar to set up time blocks effectively:

1. **Choose a Time View**
   Google Calendar's "Day" or "Week" view is best suited for time blocking, as it gives a detailed breakdown of each hour.

2. **Add Tasks as Events**
   Treat each task or activity as an event.

   o **Title:** Be specific, e.g., "Write Project Report" instead of "Work."

- o **Time Duration:** Allocate realistic time slots based on task complexity.

- o **Description:** Include relevant notes or links for quick reference.

3. **Use Color Coding**
   Assign different colors to types of tasks for visual clarity. For example:

   - o Red: Urgent tasks

   - o Blue: Meetings

   - o Green: Personal activities

4. **Include Buffers Between Tasks**
   Avoid back-to-back scheduling by adding 5-15 minutes between tasks. Use this time to transition, reflect, or take short breaks.

Time Blocking Strategies

To make your time blocking system more effective, consider the following approaches:

1. **Themed**   **Days**
   Dedicate specific days to particular types of work. For instance:

   - o Mondays for planning and administrative tasks.

   - o Tuesdays and Thursdays for deep focus work.

   - o Fridays for reflection and preparation for the next week.

2. **The Pomodoro Technique**
   Combine time blocking with the Pomodoro technique by scheduling blocks of 25 minutes for focused work followed by 5-minute breaks.

3. **Batch Similar Tasks**
   Group similar tasks together to minimize context switching. For example, block an hour for responding to emails rather than scattering this task throughout the day.

4. **Morning vs. Evening Blocks**
   Schedule high-energy, complex tasks during your peak productivity hours and routine or low-energy tasks during slower periods.

Adapting and Refining Your Time Blocks

Time blocking is not a rigid system. To ensure its effectiveness:

1. **Review and Adjust Regularly**
   At the end of each day or week, review your calendar to see what worked and what didn't. Adjust your blocks to reflect realistic expectations.

2. **Be Flexible**
   Life is unpredictable, so leave room for adjustments. Use Google Calendar's drag-and-drop feature to easily move time blocks when necessary.

3. **Track Your Progress**
   Use Google Calendar's search or "Insights" (if available) to track how much time you're spending on different activities.

4. **Avoid Overloading**
   Don't cram too many tasks into one day. Over-scheduling can lead to burnout.

Tips for Maintaining Work-Life Balance

Time blocking isn't just for work. Use it to ensure personal and leisure activities get the attention they deserve:

1. **Schedule Personal Time**
   Block time for hobbies, exercise, and family. Treat these blocks as sacred as work commitments.

2. **Plan for Breaks and Downtime**
   Regular breaks improve focus and productivity. Schedule a lunch break and smaller breaks throughout the day.

3. **Respect Boundaries**
   Clearly define the start and end of your workday. Use Google Calendar to set reminders to wind down.

Tools and Features to Enhance Time Blocking

Google Calendar offers several features to enhance your time-blocking efforts:

1. **Goals Feature**
   Use this to schedule recurring personal goals, such as exercising or learning a new skill. Google Calendar will automatically find time for these based on your availability.

2. **Recurring Events**
   Set up recurring time blocks for activities you perform daily, weekly, or monthly.

3. **Event Notifications**
   Customize reminders to alert you before tasks or blocks begin.

4. **Integrations with Other Apps**
   Sync Google Calendar with tools like Asana, Trello, or Notion to link tasks directly to your schedule.

Conclusion

Time blocking with Google Calendar is a transformative approach to managing your time and energy. By assigning purpose to every hour of your day, you can align your actions with your priorities and create a sustainable, balanced routine. Whether you're juggling a demanding job, personal commitments, or both, this method empowers you to make the most of your time while avoiding burnout.

In the next section, we'll explore how to use Google Calendar's insights to prioritize tasks effectively and further streamline your daily workflow.

7.2 Prioritizing Tasks with Calendar Insights

Managing your time effectively requires not just scheduling tasks but also identifying which tasks should take precedence. Google Calendar offers features and strategies that help you analyze your schedule and prioritize your activities to align with your goals. By utilizing calendar insights, you can achieve better focus, reduce stress, and make the most of your day.

Understanding Calendar Insights

Calendar insights are patterns and trends revealed by analyzing your events and schedules. They provide valuable data about:

- How you're allocating your time.

- Which tasks dominate your schedule.

- How often you're overbooking yourself.

By reflecting on this data, you can make informed decisions about adjustments to optimize productivity and balance.

Setting Clear Priorities

The first step in prioritizing tasks is understanding the difference between **urgent** and **important** activities. This distinction can guide how you use Google Calendar effectively.

- **Urgent Tasks**: Tasks that require immediate attention but may not contribute to long-term goals.

- **Important Tasks**: Activities that drive long-term progress but may not have immediate deadlines.

Actionable Tip: Use Google Calendar to differentiate these categories. For instance, assign distinct colors to urgent tasks (e.g., red) and important tasks (e.g., blue).

Steps to Prioritize Tasks

1. **Audit Your Current Schedule**

   o Review past weeks in your Google Calendar.

   o Identify tasks or meetings that consumed significant time without adding value.

   o Look for patterns, such as time wasted on recurring low-priority events.

Example: If a weekly meeting consistently feels unproductive, consider whether it can be replaced by an email update.

2. **Use Calendar Analytics Tools**
   Google Calendar integrates with tools like Google Workspace Insights, which provides analytics on how your time is spent. These insights can help you evaluate your current allocation of hours.

3. **Create a Task Priority Matrix**
   Apply the **Eisenhower Matrix** to your Google Calendar:

   o **Quadrant 1**: Urgent & Important – Tasks to schedule immediately.

   o **Quadrant 2**: Important but Not Urgent – Tasks to plan for proactive progress.

   o **Quadrant 3**: Urgent but Not Important – Tasks to delegate or reduce.

   o **Quadrant 4**: Neither Urgent Nor Important – Tasks to eliminate.

4. **Leverage Goals and Objectives**
   Use Google Calendar's **Goals** feature to set priorities around personal or professional development, like daily exercise or learning sessions. These activities should align with your broader objectives.

Practical Features for Prioritizing

Google Calendar offers specific features that support task prioritization:

1. **Event Descriptions and Details**
   Use the description field to outline why a task matters and what outcomes you expect.

- o   Add key deliverables or deadlines.

- o   Include links to related documents or resources.

2. **Notifications and Reminders**

- o   Schedule reminders for priority tasks at optimal intervals to avoid missing deadlines.

- o   Adjust notification settings for less important tasks to minimize distractions.

3. **Recurring Events with Adjustments**

- o   Reassess the importance of recurring tasks.

- o   Use the "edit only this instance" option to skip or modify non-essential occurrences.

4. **Event Color Coding**
   Google Calendar's color-coding system helps visually distinguish high-priority events.
   Example: Use bright colors for critical deadlines and muted tones for routine activities.

Strategies for Better Prioritization

1. **Time Blocking for High-Impact Work**
   Dedicate specific blocks of time to your most important tasks. Schedule these blocks during your peak productivity hours, and protect them from interruptions.
   Example: Mark 9:00 AM–11:00 AM for strategic planning, and disable notifications during this time.

2. **Plan Buffer Time**
   Overcommitting can lead to stress and inefficiency. Incorporate 15–30 minutes of buffer time between tasks or meetings to regroup and prepare.

3. **Regular Calendar Reviews**

- o   Conduct a weekly review of your calendar.

- Move low-priority tasks to less demanding time slots or delegate them.

- Identify tasks that should take priority in the upcoming week.

4. **Batch Similar Tasks**
   Group related tasks to minimize context-switching and improve focus. For instance, schedule all email replies during a single block instead of scattering them throughout the day.

Avoiding Overprioritization Pitfalls

While prioritizing is crucial, overprioritization can lead to micromanagement or unnecessary stress. Balance is key.

- Avoid overanalyzing every task.

- Keep flexibility for unexpected opportunities or challenges.

- Remember to prioritize downtime to recharge.

Examples of Effective Prioritization

1. **Case Study: Project Management**
   A marketing manager uses Google Calendar to plan a product launch. By prioritizing milestones and team meetings with distinct colors and reminders, they ensure that key deadlines are met without overloading their team.

2. **Case Study: Work-Life Balance**
   A busy parent blocks evenings for family time in their Google Calendar, ensuring that professional priorities do not overshadow personal commitments.

Tools and Integrations to Enhance Prioritization

1. **Google Keep**

   - Sync to-do lists with your calendar.

     o   Prioritize tasks directly in your events.

2. **Trello or Asana**
   Integrate these project management tools with Google Calendar to ensure deadlines and tasks are reflected in your schedule.

3. **Zapier Automations**
   Automate repetitive tasks, such as transferring emails with action items directly into your calendar as events.

Conclusion

Prioritizing tasks with Google Calendar allows you to align your time with your goals while maintaining flexibility. By leveraging its features and adopting effective strategies, you can transform your schedule into a tool for success. Regularly reflect on your priorities, adapt your calendar to evolving needs, and enjoy the benefits of a well-organized life.

7.3 Setting Boundaries and Preventing Overcommitment

In today's fast-paced world, the lines between work and personal life can blur, especially with the ease of access to digital tools like Google Calendar. Setting boundaries is crucial to maintaining a healthy work-life balance and preventing burnout. Google Calendar can be a powerful ally in this effort, providing not only the structure you need to organize your time but also the tools to set clear limits and prioritize your well-being.

The Importance of Boundaries

Boundaries are limits we set in our personal and professional lives to define how we interact with others and manage our time. They help protect our time and energy, ensuring that we are able to focus on the activities that truly matter to us. In the context of work and life, boundaries allow you to:

1. **Manage Time Effectively:** Boundaries help you define when you're working and when you're not, allowing for dedicated time for personal pursuits, family, and relaxation.

2. **Protect Mental Health:** Without boundaries, constant work demands can lead to stress, anxiety, and burnout. Having time for self-care is essential.

3. **Improve Productivity:** When you set boundaries, you're better able to focus on important tasks without distraction, increasing your overall efficiency.

4. **Enhance Relationships:** Setting boundaries allows you to spend quality time with loved ones, ensuring that you're present and engaged when you're not working.

Google Calendar offers a wide array of features to help you establish and enforce these boundaries. By effectively managing your calendar, you can avoid overcommitment and create a schedule that respects your time and energy.

1. Define Your Work Hours and Personal Time

The first step in setting boundaries is to establish clear distinctions between work and personal time. Google Calendar allows you to color-code your events and block off specific time slots for work and non-work activities.

Setting Work Hours

The first key boundary to set is your work hours. These are the times when you are actively engaged in professional tasks, and it's essential to be mindful about what you accept during these hours. To do this:

- **Create a Work Calendar:** Consider setting up a separate calendar for work-related activities. This will allow you to quickly identify which events are related to your job and which are personal.

- **Set Working Hours in Google Calendar:** In your Google Calendar settings, you can set your work hours, which will provide a visual cue for yourself and others when scheduling. This way, events outside these hours can be viewed as exceptions, and you can resist the temptation to schedule work late into the evening or on weekends.

- **Set Event Reminders:** To further enhance your boundaries, use reminders or pop-up alerts to notify you when an event is nearing its start time. This can help you mentally prepare and transition out of personal time to professional time without the stress of last-minute rushes.

Blocking Off Personal Time

Just as you define work hours, it's equally important to schedule personal time. This includes downtime for self-care, family time, hobbies, and relaxation. Many people overlook personal time when planning, but it's crucial to keep this space sacred to avoid overcommitment.

- **Color-Code Personal Time:** Choose a distinct color for personal events in your Google Calendar to differentiate them from work-related tasks. This visual cue will reinforce the importance of making time for yourself and help you maintain balance.

- **Use "Out of Office" Events:** When you're unavailable for work-related events or meetings, set "Out of Office" status in Google Calendar. This lets others know that you are not available, preventing them from overloading your calendar.

- **Treat Personal Time as Non-Negotiable:** Be intentional about treating personal time as a priority, just as you would a business meeting or work deadline. This will help prevent the feeling that you're "too busy" to enjoy downtime or take care of yourself.

2. Prioritize Your Commitments

One of the main reasons people overcommit is that they don't prioritize effectively. Google Calendar offers several tools to help you manage and prioritize your schedule:

Use Event Descriptions and Notes

When scheduling events, use the description field to clarify the purpose of the event and any necessary preparation. This will help you decide whether this commitment aligns with your priorities or if it can be delegated to someone else. By clearly identifying the value of each event, you can make better decisions about where to invest your time.

Set Time Blocks for Important Tasks

Time blocking is a strategy where you allocate specific blocks of time for certain tasks or categories of activities. For example, you could block time for focused work, meetings, or creative brainstorming. You can then ensure that each of these time blocks is aligned with your goals, preventing overcommitment.

- **Time Blocking for Focused Work:** Reserve time in your calendar for uninterrupted focus on important tasks. Use reminders to signal when you need to start or stop these blocks, and try to avoid adding meetings or appointments during this time.

- **Buffer Time Between Events:** Schedule buffer time between meetings to avoid the temptation to take on too many tasks in one day. A 10–15 minute break between events allows you to reset and refocus.

Use Google Calendar's Task Feature

Google Calendar integrates with Google Tasks, allowing you to add tasks directly into your calendar. These tasks can be prioritized by importance and deadline, ensuring you're focusing on what matters most. Prioritize your to-do list and assign a specific time in your calendar to each task, helping you avoid taking on too much at once.

- **Break Large Tasks into Smaller Steps:** Large tasks can feel overwhelming and lead to overcommitment. Break these tasks down into manageable steps and allocate specific time slots to work on them. By focusing on smaller pieces, you can prevent the stress of having too much on your plate at once.

3. Set Boundaries with Others

Often, overcommitment is driven by external expectations, whether from coworkers, friends, or family. Setting boundaries with others is crucial to maintaining a balanced schedule.

Communicate Clearly

Google Calendar allows you to share your calendar with colleagues, clients, or family members. Be transparent about your availability and boundaries:

- **Share Your Calendar:** Share your work calendar with others, allowing them to see when you're free or busy. This can prevent unnecessary scheduling conflicts or last-minute requests that could disrupt your balance.

- **Set Expectations:** Use the "Out of Office" or "Busy" status on Google Calendar to clearly communicate when you're unavailable. This signals to others that you are off-limits for work-related matters during certain periods, such as evenings, weekends, or personal time.

Set Limits on Meeting Times

It's easy to overcommit when meetings run longer than expected or when you say "yes" to every meeting request. To avoid this, set strict limits on your meeting times and stick to them.

- **Time-Capped Meetings:** Block specific time limits for meetings on your calendar, and ensure everyone is aware of these boundaries. For example, limit internal meetings to 30 minutes and external meetings to an hour. This will help you maintain control over your time.

- **Decline Unnecessary Invitations:** Don't be afraid to decline meeting invitations that are outside your priority areas or are unnecessary for your role. Google Calendar allows you to quickly respond with an "Accept" or "Decline" button, so you can be selective about the events you choose to attend.

Use Google Calendar to Enforce "No-Work" Zones

If you often find yourself working during personal time, it's time to establish non-negotiable "no-work" zones. Google Calendar can help you schedule and enforce these boundaries:

- **Set Non-Work Time Blocks:** Schedule personal events, like family dinners, relaxation, or exercise, and mark them as "Busy." This reinforces the importance of taking time off and prevents others from scheduling over these blocks.

- **Turn Off Notifications During Personal Time:** When you're off the clock, turn off email, chat, and calendar notifications to disconnect from work. Google Calendar allows you to manage these notifications and reduce distractions, helping you stay focused during non-work hours.

4. Recognize and Manage Overcommitment

Despite our best efforts, there will be times when we inadvertently overcommit. Recognizing the signs of overcommitment early is key to preventing burnout.

Warning Signs of Overcommitment

- **Physical Symptoms:** Feeling fatigued, stressed, or burned out are signs that you might have taken on too much. Listen to your body and pay attention to mental health indicators, like anxiety or irritability.

- **Back-to-Back Events:** If your calendar is filled with back-to-back meetings with no time for breaks, it's a sign that you need to reassess your time management. Try spreading out your meetings to allow space for self-care.

- **Neglecting Personal Time:** If you're skipping meals, exercise, or time with loved ones to meet work demands, it's time to reset your boundaries.

Dealing with Overcommitment

When you recognize that you're overcommitted, take immediate steps to adjust your calendar. Google Calendar allows you to easily reschedule or delegate events to others. Reassess your priorities and identify which commitments can be postponed or removed.

- **Delegate Tasks:** If you're overwhelmed, delegate tasks to others, if possible. Google Calendar enables you to share events and tasks with colleagues, allowing them to take over certain responsibilities.

- **Reschedule and Refocus:** Don't hesitate to move events around to create breathing room in your schedule. By rescheduling, you regain control over your time.

In conclusion, setting boundaries and preventing overcommitment requires discipline and clear intention, but with the right tools, it becomes an achievable goal. Google Calendar can help you organize and manage your time in a way that respects your personal boundaries and professional obligations. By setting clear boundaries, prioritizing your commitments, and staying mindful of your energy levels, you can achieve a better work-life balance

and avoid the pitfalls of overcommitment.

Conclusion

8.1 Recap of Key Takeaways

Google Calendar is more than just a scheduling tool; it is a versatile system for organizing your life, improving productivity, and reducing the stress associated with managing time. Over the course of this guide, we have explored its features in-depth, uncovering ways to make the most of this powerful tool. Here's a detailed recap of the key takeaways to help reinforce what you've learned and ensure you can apply these principles effectively.

Understanding the Basics

One of the first steps in mastering Google Calendar is becoming familiar with its interface and core functionalities. Whether you're using it on your computer or mobile device, the platform offers intuitive options to view and manage your schedule. The calendar views, such as Day, Week, and Month, provide flexibility depending on how detailed or broad your perspective needs to be. Syncing across devices ensures that your schedule is always up-to-date and accessible wherever you are.

Creating and Managing Events

Adding events is the cornerstone of using Google Calendar effectively. We covered how to create new events with specific titles, dates, times, and even additional details such as locations and descriptions. The ability to customize events with recurrence patterns, color codes, and attachments ensures your calendar is not only informative but visually organized.

Managing events doesn't stop at creation. Editing, rescheduling, or canceling events is straightforward, allowing you to adjust to changes effortlessly. Google Calendar's notification system ensures you stay on top of your commitments without feeling overwhelmed.

Leveraging Advanced Features

Google Calendar shines when you dive into its advanced features. Appointment slots enable you to create structured availability for others to book time with you, a particularly useful tool for professionals managing meetings. Similarly, reminders and tasks help ensure you stay productive, focusing on both small to-do items and larger projects.

Collaboration is made easy through shared calendars and event invitations. These tools streamline communication and coordination, especially for teams or families managing group activities. Adding public holidays, sports schedules, or importing calendars from other sources further enriches your planning capabilities.

Customization and Settings

Personalizing Google Calendar to suit your needs is a game-changer. Adjusting settings such as time zones, default notifications, and working hours allows the platform to align with your daily routine. Creating multiple calendars—whether for work, personal life, or hobbies—provides clarity and prevents your schedule from feeling cluttered.

Custom overlays and color-coding make it easy to differentiate between categories at a glance, ensuring you maintain a balanced overview of your commitments. Syncing with external sources, such as other calendars or apps, helps you centralize all your planning in one place.

Integrations and Automation

Google Calendar's ability to integrate with other tools makes it an indispensable part of any digital ecosystem. Seamlessly working with Gmail, Google Meet, and third-party apps ensures that event scheduling and participation are smooth processes.

Smart device integration allows you to manage your calendar via voice commands or receive updates on wearable devices. Automation tools, such as Google Workspace add-ons or APIs, further extend its capabilities, enabling you to save time and minimize repetitive tasks.

Efficiency Tips

Maximizing your efficiency with Google Calendar is all about leveraging hidden features and adopting best practices. Keyboard shortcuts, for example, can drastically reduce the time spent navigating the interface. Other underutilized features, such as attaching meeting notes directly to events or embedding video conferencing links, streamline workflows.

We also addressed common challenges, such as resolving syncing errors and managing overlapping events, ensuring you can troubleshoot effectively when issues arise.

Work-Life Balance

One of the most impactful uses of Google Calendar is its ability to promote a balanced lifestyle. By applying techniques such as time blocking, prioritizing important tasks, and setting boundaries with dedicated personal time, you can maintain a healthy equilibrium between work and leisure.

Using insights from your calendar, such as weekly summaries or task completion rates, helps you identify areas for improvement. These adjustments make it easier to stay organized without overcommitting or burning out.

Building a Sustainable Routine

Ultimately, the true value of Google Calendar lies in its ability to help you build sustainable habits. It's not just about managing your time today but creating systems that support long-term productivity and well-being. Whether you're planning personal milestones, professional goals, or daily errands, Google Calendar can be your constant companion in achieving a more organized life.

Final Reflections

As we wrap up this guide, it's clear that Google Calendar is not merely a scheduling app— it's a versatile tool that adapts to your unique needs. By applying the strategies and techniques covered in this book, you can take control of your time, reduce stress, and pave the way for a more productive and fulfilling life.

Take a moment to reflect on what you've learned and how you can implement it into your daily routine. Remember, the key to mastering Google Calendar is consistency. The more you use it, the more intuitive and effective it will become.

In the next section, we'll offer some final thoughts and share additional resources to help you continue learning and enhancing your organizational skills.

8.2 Final Thoughts on Staying Organized

In today's fast-paced world, staying organized is no longer a luxury but a necessity. Effective organization not only helps you manage your daily responsibilities but also provides the mental clarity and focus needed to achieve your long-term goals. Google Calendar, with its vast array of features, serves as a powerful ally in this journey. In this final section, we'll explore the deeper impact of staying organized, strategies to maintain your systems, and how Google Calendar can continue to support your success.

1. The Value of Staying Organized

Staying organized offers countless benefits beyond simply keeping track of appointments. It allows you to:

- **Reduce Stress**: Knowing that everything is accounted for in your calendar reduces the mental load of remembering tasks and deadlines.

- **Enhance Productivity**: By structuring your day effectively, you can focus on high-priority tasks without distractions.

- **Build Consistency**: An organized schedule helps you develop positive habits and routines, contributing to personal and professional growth.

- **Improve Relationships**: Honoring commitments and managing time well reflects positively on how others perceive you, strengthening trust and collaboration.

2. Common Challenges and How to Overcome Them

Even with the best intentions, staying organized can be challenging. Here are some common obstacles and how to address them:

- **Overcommitment**: It's tempting to say yes to every opportunity, but this can lead to burnout. Use Google Calendar to block out personal time and set boundaries for your commitments.

- **Procrastination**: Tasks often seem daunting when they're not broken down into manageable steps. Use Google Calendar's task feature to divide larger projects into smaller, actionable items.

- **Distractions**: The digital world is full of interruptions. Schedule focus time in your calendar and minimize notifications to stay on track.

- **Neglecting Self-Care**: Amidst busy schedules, personal well-being is often overlooked. Schedule regular breaks and activities that rejuvenate you, such as exercise, meditation, or hobbies.

3. Strategies for Long-Term Organization

To stay consistently organized, it's essential to establish sustainable habits. Consider the following strategies:

- **Conduct Weekly Reviews**: Dedicate time each week to review your upcoming schedule, reflect on accomplishments, and adjust plans as needed.

- **Prioritize Flexibility**: Life is unpredictable, and plans often change. Use Google Calendar's drag-and-drop feature to easily reschedule tasks and events without losing track.

- **Leverage Automation**: Use integrations with tools like Google Tasks, Zapier, or Trello to automate repetitive tasks and streamline your workflow.

- **Declutter Regularly**: Over time, your calendar may become cluttered with outdated events or reminders. Periodically clean up your calendar to maintain clarity.

- **Stay Educated**: Google Calendar continues to evolve, introducing new features and enhancements. Keep up-to-date with updates to make the most of the tool.

4. The Role of Reflection

Staying organized is not just about planning but also about reflecting on what works and what doesn't. Take time to assess your scheduling habits and consider:

- **What are my top priorities?**

- **Am I allocating time effectively to these priorities?**

- **Are there recurring inefficiencies in my routine?**

- **How can I adjust my calendar to better align with my goals?**

Reflection helps you refine your approach to organization, ensuring that your calendar remains a tool that serves your evolving needs.

5. Using Google Calendar as a Holistic Tool

Google Calendar is more than just a scheduling tool; it's a hub for managing your life. To maximize its potential:

- **Combine Personal and Professional Calendars**: Create separate calendars for work, family, and personal goals but view them together to ensure a balanced schedule.

- **Use Color Coding**: Assign different colors to specific types of events or tasks for quick visual recognition.

- **Integrate with Other Tools**: Sync your calendar with apps like Google Drive, Zoom, or Slack to streamline your workflow.

- **Enable Notifications Strategically**: Set reminders for critical tasks or events to ensure you never miss an important deadline.

6. The Bigger Picture

Ultimately, staying organized is about creating space for what matters most. By managing your time effectively, you can focus on activities that bring fulfillment and joy. Whether it's spending quality time with loved ones, pursuing a passion project, or excelling in your career, organization empowers you to live a life aligned with your values.

Google Calendar acts as a reliable partner in this process, helping you navigate the complexities of modern life with ease. Embrace its features, adapt them to your unique needs, and remember that organization is an ongoing journey, not a destination.

Final Encouragement

As you continue using Google Calendar, remember to stay patient and flexible. Organization is a skill that improves with practice, and there will be days when things don't go as planned. When this happens, revisit your calendar, make adjustments, and keep moving forward.

Your calendar is a reflection of your priorities and aspirations. Treat it with care, and it will become a powerful tool to support your success, happiness, and well-being.

8.3 Additional Resources for Continued Learning

Mastering Google Calendar is just the beginning of your journey to becoming more organized and efficient. To truly integrate this tool into your daily routine, and to maximize its potential, continuous learning and exploration of related tools and techniques are essential. Below, we'll dive into a variety of resources to deepen your knowledge and help you become a pro at planning your life with ease.

Online Tutorials and Video Guides

One of the easiest ways to continue learning is by watching online tutorials. Platforms like YouTube, Udemy, and Coursera offer free and paid courses on Google Calendar, ranging from beginner-friendly guides to advanced techniques.

- **YouTube Channels**: Many content creators regularly post Google Calendar tips and tricks. Search for "Google Calendar productivity hacks" or "Google Calendar tutorial" to find videos that match your skill level.

- **Udemy and Coursera**: These platforms often host in-depth courses on using Google Workspace tools, including Google Calendar. Look for courses with high ratings and comprehensive syllabi that cover integrations, time management strategies, and practical use cases.

Google's Official Support and Training Resources

Google provides extensive documentation and training tools to help users understand its products.

- **Google Help Center**: The Google Calendar Help Center offers step-by-step guides on setting up and troubleshooting features. It's an excellent resource for addressing specific issues or learning about new features.

- **Google Workspace Learning Center**: This platform provides interactive tutorials and use-case scenarios to help users get the most out of Google Calendar and other Google Workspace tools.

- **Product Updates and Release Notes**: Regularly check Google's official blog or release notes to stay updated on new features and enhancements.

Books on Productivity and Time Management

Google Calendar is a tool, but its effectiveness largely depends on how well you manage your time. Reading books about time management and productivity can provide frameworks and strategies to complement your use of Google Calendar.

- **"Atomic Habits" by James Clear**: Learn how small changes in your habits can significantly impact your time management.

- **"The 7 Habits of Highly Effective People" by Stephen Covey**: This classic book provides a roadmap for personal and professional effectiveness, including strategies for prioritizing tasks.

- **"Make Time" by Jake Knapp and John Zeratsky**: Focuses on practical techniques for making the most of your time, which you can easily implement using Google Calendar.

Podcasts and Webinars

Listening to podcasts or attending webinars can expose you to diverse perspectives and advanced strategies for managing your time and calendar effectively.

- **Podcasts**:
  - *The Productivity Show*: Offers actionable tips on time management, scheduling, and productivity tools.

  - *Getting Things Done*: Based on David Allen's methodology, this podcast emphasizes planning and execution strategies that can be adapted to Google Calendar.

- **Webinars**: Many tech companies and productivity experts host free webinars on using digital tools for time management. Look out for live sessions or recorded webinars from Google or third-party organizations.

Joining Online Communities

Engaging with online communities can provide support, inspiration, and ideas for using Google Calendar more effectively.

- **Reddit**: Subreddits like r/productivity and r/GoogleCalendar are great places to ask questions, share tips, and learn from other users.

- **Facebook Groups and LinkedIn**: Search for groups focused on productivity, digital tools, or Google Workspace users.

- **Forums**: Platforms like Quora or Google's own user forums often host discussions on advanced use cases and problem-solving tips for Google Calendar.

Productivity Apps and Integrations

To extend the functionality of Google Calendar, explore third-party apps and integrations that work seamlessly with it.

- **Task Management Tools**: Integrate tools like Todoist, Trello, or Asana to streamline task management alongside your calendar events.

- **Automation Platforms**: Use Zapier or IFTTT to automate repetitive tasks, such as sending reminders or syncing events across calendars.

- **Focus and Time-Tracking Apps**: Apps like Toggl or RescueTime can help you track how you spend your time and adjust your calendar accordingly.

Workshops and Professional Training

For those who want to dive deeper, attending workshops or enrolling in professional training programs can be immensely beneficial.

- **Google Workspace Certification**: If you want to become an expert in Google tools, consider pursuing a certification. Google offers courses for individuals who want to master their suite of apps, including Google Calendar.

- **Corporate Training Programs**: Many organizations provide training on productivity tools, including hands-on sessions for mastering Google Calendar.

Experimenting with New Features

Google Calendar frequently rolls out updates and new features. Staying curious and exploring these features can enhance your experience.

- Try experimenting with **Time Insights** to understand how you spend your days.

- Use **Focus Time** to block distractions and stay productive.

- Explore **appointment scheduling** to streamline meeting bookings without back-and-forth emails.

Building a Personalized System

Finally, the most effective way to learn is by doing. Customize Google Calendar to suit your unique needs:

- Develop a **color-coding system** for work, personal, and family events.

- Create **templates for recurring tasks or meetings**.

- Experiment with different views (e.g., weekly vs. daily) to find what works best for your planning style.

Staying Curious and Open to Learning

Remember, learning doesn't stop once you master the basics. New tools, integrations, and strategies are always emerging. Stay curious, seek feedback, and adapt your system as your needs evolve.

By taking advantage of these resources and continuously refining your skills, you'll not only master Google Calendar but also elevate your overall productivity and time management. This journey is about progress, not perfection—so keep exploring and enjoying the process

Acknowledgment

Thank you so much for choosing to purchase Google Calendar Essentials: Plan Your Life with Ease.

I am deeply grateful for your support and trust in this book as a resource to help you become more organized, productive, and in control of your time. Writing this guide has been a labor of love, and knowing it's in the hands of readers like you makes the effort worthwhile.

Whether you are just starting with Google Calendar or looking to enhance your skills, my hope is that this book will empower you to achieve your goals with greater clarity and ease. Your time is valuable, and I am honored to be a small part of your journey toward living a more organized and balanced life.

If this book has helped you in any way, I would love to hear your feedback. Sharing your experience not only helps me improve but also inspires others to take that first step toward better time management.

Once again, thank you for your support and for allowing me to guide you through this journey. Wishing you all the best in mastering your schedule and making the most of every moment!

Warm regards,

www.ingramcontent.com/pod-product-compliance
Lightning Source LLC
La Vergne TN
LVHW062317060326
832902LV00013B/2261